¥950

¥980

ス ¥980

当店オリジナルの
HONEY & ONION
ドレッシングを使った ¥630
FRESHな
サラダです！
ドレッシングのお持ち帰りもどうぞ！

LUNC
TIM
限定

NEW

00で
ン
白)

TOKYO

A pocket guide to the city's best
cultural hangouts, shops, bars
and eateries

STEVE WIDE & MICHELLE MACKINTOSH

Hardie Grant

TRAVEL

CONTENT/

INTRODUCTION

Konnichiwa and welcome to *Tokyo Pocket Precincts*.

Tokyo is our favourite city in the world. It's a place of eye-popping fashion, incredible food, animal cafes, hole-in-the-wall bars and train stations as big as city blocks. There are towering buildings with neon signs next to warren-like alleys full of tiny, old-world eateries and the shopping is dangerous! You'll be cramming your bags with toys, the latest gadgets, homewares and beautiful crafts. There is so much to love here, and we hope you'll uncover your own treasured places.

Tokyo is a gigantic metropolis made up of smaller cities, each with their own unique feel. If you tackle Tokyo one part at a time, you'll quickly get a handle on it.

This is your pocket guide to 15 of Tokyo's best precincts, and for each we've picked our must-do shopping, eating, drinking and cultural experiences. There are also suggestions for the best trips out of Tokyo. This is our personal take on the city, which we hope you can use as a springboard for your own adventures.

We've included train station exit information for each place and useful maps at the back of the book (*see* p. 190) to help you find your way (it's easy to get lost). You'll also find some handy tips on navigating Tokyo, etiquette, food, drinks and more travel tips (*see* p. 184).

So launch yourself into Tokyo's precincts. Once you get your bearings there is no end to the fun, amazing shopping and eating, friendly people and unforgettable adventures. There is simply no other place in the world like Tokyo, and we hope you love it as much as we do.

Steve and Michelle

A PERFECT TOKYO DAY

There are hundreds of perfect Tokyo days. Sometimes an unplanned day, drifting off the grid, is amazing.

Up early? Head to **Yoyogi Park** for a jog and visit the **Meiji Shrine** to start off the day in a spiritual way. The shrine opens at 5am, magical as the sun creeps through the clouds. Shibuya's shopping is unmissable for the latest fashion, music, gadgets, homewares and general trends. **Loft**, **Tokyu Hands** and **Hikarie ShinQs** will satisfy the most hardcore shopper. Stroll along **Cat Street**, browsing small boutiques and vintage fashion, before emerging onto bustling **Omotesando Dori**. A delicious tonkatsu (deep-friend pork cutlet) lunch awaits at **Maisen**, and nearby **Koffee Mameya** serves up some of the city's best brews. Head up to Harajuku with its swarming crowds and arresting fashions, or down to Aoyama for art and design at **Spiral Design Market**, and some of the world's finest retail architecture including **Prada**, and **Comme des Garçons**. Pop into **Higashiya Man** for wagashi (Japanese sweets), before making your way down to the serene **Nezu Museum**.

Lose yourself in the beauty and old-world charm of Yanaka before a stroll though **Ueno Park** or a ride on one of the famous swan boats on **Shinobazu Pond**.

Head to Meguro and stroll through the beautiful building and gardens of the **Tokyo Metropolitan Teien Art Museum**.

For a breezy afternoon head to Kichijoji. Explore the design and vintage stores in Nakamichi Dori and the market stalls of the **Sun Road Arcade**.

Then, wander over to peaceful **Inokashira Park**, and the joyful **Ghibli Museum**.

As the light fades, head to Roppongi and ride the elevator to the top of the **Mori Tower** to catch an exhibition at the **Mori Art Museum** and stunning dusk views of the city.

As hunger sets in, head to Ebisu, get amongst the salary men and fill up on beer, ramen or yakitori. **Koenji's Live Houses** will cap off your perfect day. Sit back with a beer and listen to some edgy music.

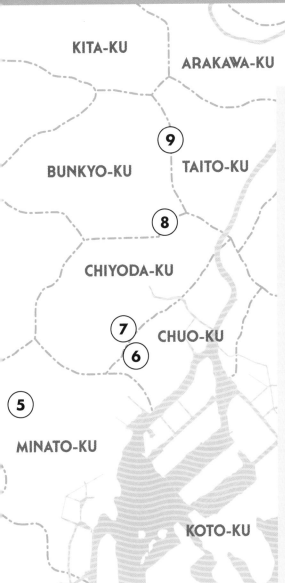

KITA-KU

ARAKAWA-KU

BUNKYO-KU

TAITO-KU

CHIYODA-KU

CHUO-KU

MINATO-KU

KOTO-KU

SHINAGAWA-KU

∫HIBUYA

With its flashing neon lights, giant TV screens and chaotic crowds, Shibuya is an up-late precinct with a serious shopping addiction, where worldwide trends, youth fashion and lifestyles are born. Shibuya Station's Hachiko Square serves as a jump-off point for exploring. To the west, you'll find everything from seedy love hotels and games parlours to some of the world's best music venues, blockbuster art and oh, did we mention serious shopping?

To the east, chic department store, Hikarie ShinQs (*see* p. 10), has brought a calm and refined air to the madness. A stroll down languid Cat Street (*see* p. 9) towards Harajuku changes the pace even more. As the TV screens and noise fall away you'll also discover a thriving network of backstreets, where coffee stands seem to sprout daily and vintage stores and edgy new fashion boutiques sit alongside Tokyo stalwarts.

→ *Shibuya Cross*

1 HACHIKO SQUARE & SHIBUYA CROSS

2-1 Dogenzaka
3463 1211
city.shibuya.tokyo.jp
Open Mon–Sun 24-hours
Shibuya station, exit 8 or
Hachiko exit
[MAP p. 192 C2]

Hachiko Square is a main Shibuya station hub, the entry point to Shibuya's hive of restless activity. The statue of Hachiko, the loyal Akita dog who waited for his master for nine years, though his master had passed away, is a potent symbol of loyalty. It's Tokyo's most popular place to meet up with friends. The statue is surprisingly modest, a small casting in bronze. You'll know it by the long line of visitors waiting to have their photo snapped beside it. The adjacent Shibuya Cross, nicknamed 'The Scramble', is one of the world's most photographed sights – and it's an intersection! When the lights turn green you can walk in any direction over five main roads and 1000 people do just that – each time. At peak times this number escalates dramatically, it's crazy. Join in the mad flurry of limbs and take your own pics of the madness before launching into vibrant Shibuya.

POCKET TIP
The alleys and lanes around Mark City are full of tiny eateries, bars and noodle joints.

2 THE YARD

Shibuya Modi building 4F
1-21-3 Jinnan, Shibuya
4336 8241
the-yard.jp
Open Mon–Sun 11am–9pm
Shibuya station, exit 6–2
[MAP p. 192 C2]

The Yard deconstruct the kimono for the 21st-century sophisticate, providing sharp tailoring for both men and women in a store with a minimalist aesthetic. Originally from Sendai, The Yard is making a name for itself in Tokyo as the modern frontier of classical Japanese dress and a serious counterpoint to Shibuya's frenzied pop culture. You can leave with everything you need for full kimono dress, layering it all up together, or use separates as modern pieces to wear with your current outfit. Swoon over their range of haori (jackets), obi and obidome (kimono sashes and accessories), zori (sandles), tabi socks and bags. Michelle never leaves without one of their beautiful hair ornaments, stand-out pieces on their own. Fabric is sold by 'the yard' and is a history lesson of skilled fiber artisans from all over the country – from naturally dyed handwoven textiles, warp and weft, yarn and weave, to interwoven linen and cottons, silk and hemp. If you're keen to immerse yourself, ask about their kimono dressing lessons.

3 GRIMOIRE

8F, Ohata building,
1-10-7 Jinnan, Shibuyaku
3780 6203
grimoire-onlineshop.com
Open Mon–Fri 1–8pm,
Sat–Sun 12pm–8pm
Shibuya station, Hachiko exit
[MAP p. 193 D1]

Grimoire will make you feel like you've dropped through the rabbit hole into the darkest parts of Wonderland to go vintage hunting with Alice. This sinister fairy forest caters to followers of the dolly-kei style: a mashup of Victorian lace, Grimm's fairytales and Gothic romance. Taxidermy, cuckoo clocks, creepy dolls, Renaissance paintings and hanging puppets all conspire to make this the haunted house of retro shopping. Search the bulging racks of frou-frou dresses, Eastern European folk clothing and goth-girl cute for finds that are way outside the box. Embroidered trimmings, floral headpieces, cameos, brooches, patterned tights and Victorian perfume bottles complete the look.

POCKET TIP
Pop into Grimoire's sister store Beryl located on the 4th floor in the same building.

4 SHIBUYA SHOPPING

Shibuya station, Hachiko exit [MAP p. 192]

Shibuya can keep even the most savvy shopper occupied for days. A good place to start is at the **Shibuya 109** building, an absolute fashion mecca, especially for the younger set.

Newcomer **Modi** offers a mix of Japanese fashion and lifestyle brands, including HMV music and books (complete with an English section). Also check out bespoke Kimono shop **The Yard** (*see* p. 3), the great range of organic cosmetics at **CosmeKitchen**, and stop for a drink at **Streamer Coffee Company** on the 6th floor. Across the road you'll find the brightly coloured retro futurism of **Tower Records**, a musical playground set over nine floors.

Jinnan is a cool enclave with casual chic fashion stores such as **Beams** (note: Beams Boy is actually a boyish girl's label), **Journal Standard** and **United Arrows**. **Tokyu Hands** (*see* p. 7) is a famous lifestyle megastore, while conjoined stores **Muji** (*see* p. 73) and **Loft** (*see* p. 62) have inspiring homewares, stationery and everyday goods. Scour this area for amazing new and vintage records, toys, manga and figurines.

POCKET TIP
Visit Journal Standard for a great selection of Japanese gifts.

5 ∫OT

5-28-7 Jingumae, Shibuyaku
5464 3677
Open Mon–Fri 12pm–8pm,
Sat–Sun 11.30am–8pm
Meiji-Jingumae station, exit 4
[MAP p. 194 B4]

Mikami Tomohiro has put his own personality into this Shibuya branch of leather-goods maker Sot. The store is a beautiful little handicraft haven just off Cat Street decorated with found furniture, tiny illustrations and wooden slab tables. You can instantly see the quality of the leather goods for sale here. Bags and shoes feature prominently, including wonderfully wrinkled shoulder totes and stylishly distressed leather footwear, which add creativity to the everyday. You can also pick up folios, wallets and a wide range of intricate creations, such as the 'multipurpose leather case', a round coin purse that you can hang from your bag. Prices reflect the quality of the products.

6 TOKYU HANDS

12-18 Udagawacho Shibuyaku
5489 5111
tokyu-hands.co.jp
Open Mon–Sun 10am–9pm
Shibuya station, Hachiko exit
[MAP p. 192 B1]

'When you visit, you find what you want' is the Tokyu Hands catchcry. Indeed, the range of homewares, stationery and travel goods here will have you wondering just when your shopping is going to stop. There's plenty here to enhance your lifestyle, but Tokyu Hands' main job is to inspire you to style up your kitchen, choose the perfect umbrella or camping gear, put together a sticker album or get involved in just about any kind of DIY project you can think of. The ridiculously extensive range caters for hobbyists, handy-men and -women and professionals alike. If you've ever wanted to do it yourself, your journey starts here. If you haven't, don't be surprised if you come out of Tokyu Hands with a sudden passion for quilting or home renovation.

POCKET TIP
Grab some friends and head into a purika (photo booth) to take some fun hyper-real pics.

7 TOKYU FOOD SHOW

2-24-1 Dogenzaka, Shibuyaku
3477 3111
tokyu-dept.co.jp/toyoko/
foodshow
Open Mon–Sun 10am–8pm
Shibuya station, Hachiko exit
[MAP p.193 D3]

You'll never think of shopping-centre food halls in the same way again after spending a few hours gawking at the variety of food on display in this basement hawkers' market. It's crazy at any time of the day, but things really get crowded when work is over and Tokyoites want to grab something to take home. The offerings run from Japanese and international street food to upmarket fare. Even the fussiest of eaters will be happy here, as there's just so much to choose from, including a great gyoza (dumpling) stand, rice-cracker stalls, sweets vendors and all manner of sushi, sashimi, grilled meats and rice dishes. There are free samples galore so you can try before you buy. Hit the food hall at closing time for some seriously marked-down bargains.

POCKET TIP
Use one of the refrigerated lockers in Tokyu Food Show's food hall to store your purchases if you want to keep shopping.

8 CAT STREET

Shibuya or Meiji-jingumae station
[MAP p. 194 C3]

Cat Street connects Shibuya with Harajuku, and it's purrrrrfect (and nearly car free) for a casual stroll or cycle. There's always a photo shoot or a TV vox pop going on. It's a mix of eateries and coffee joints, boutique versions of name brands and small independent fashion labels. **Nozy Coffee** gives you the fuel you'll need, **G.B Gafas** makes sophisticated spectacles in contemporary styles, while **Bulle De Savon** has chic, quirky clothes for the stylish girl-about-Tokyo. Further up the street you'll find **Ragtag** who recycle designer clothing. If you need a snack, head to **Wara Tako**, a sliver of a building housing a charming stand serving up tasty takoyaki (fried octopus in batter), queue up at **Luke's Lobster** or delve into the divine dumplings at **Gyoza-ro**. In the backstreets hunt out **Art Style Market** for curious vintage, and vast mod cavern **Fred Perry** has sharp Japanese-only versions of the iconic English label. Sleek retail enclave **The Gyre Building** features **1LDK Depot**, **the Moma Museum Shop** and **Trading Museum by Comme Des Garçons**. From here flow out into vibrant Omotesando dori.

9 HIKARIE ƧHINQƧ

Shibuya Hikarie ShinQs
2-21-1 Shibuya, Shibuya
5468 5892
hikarie.jp
Open Mon–Sun 10am–9pm
(department store); 11am–11pm
(restaurants)
Shibuya station, exit 15
[MAP p. 193 D3]

Hikarie ShinQs brings together Tokyo's best design retailers, galleries, cafes and restaurants in a concept department store over 11 floors. Stand-outs include **Margaret Howell**, **Beams Light** and **45R** for up-to-date fashion, and **Smith** for retro-inspired stationery and gadgetry. **Collex**, **Idée** and **Claska** all have unique, beautiful everyday household items. The eighth floor features **D&Department**'s design store and gallery, the **D47 Museum**, showcasing Japanese beauty and ingenuity in design and craft. After shopping, stop at **D47 Shokudo** for home comfort food. Enjoy one of their regional sake tasting sets while taking in the stunning view of **Shibuya Cross** (*see* p. 2). Or stock up in the excellent food hall on the two basement levels. On floors six and seven, it's more about sit-down dining. Don't miss Kyoto's **Satei Zenkashoin** on the fifth floor – a tea and sweets specialist.

POCKET TIP
If it's raining outside, you can use the Shibuya station overpass to access Hikarie.

10 SATEI HATO

1-15-19 Shibuya, Shibuyaku
3400 9088
Open Mon–Sun 11am–11.30pm
Shibuya station, east exit
[MAP p. 193 D2]

Kissaten (classic coffee houses) were all over Japan in the '50s and '60s, but now they're relatively few and far between. When you step into the kissaten Satei Hato, the world outside ceases to exist and time stands still. Its interior is a mishmash of European antiques, dark wood and Chinese designs, and low lighting and classical music add to the days-of-yore allure. You won't get latte art here, but you will get a warm welcome from genial host Toyoshi Taguchi, who's been working at Satei Hato since 1989. Grab a seat at the bar and he'll choose a cup to suit your personality from the great wall of china behind him. You'll be mesmerised as you watch him make your coffee – it's like witnessing a master craftsman in action. Order the chiffon cake with maple icing for a superb accompaniment to your brew. You're paying for the perfect blend in an exquisite cup in a beautiful setting here – so the coffee is a little more pricey than usual, around ¥600 to ¥1000 per cup – but it's worth it for this thoroughly unique Tokyo experience.

11 TOFU CUISINE SORANO

4-17 Sakuragaokacho,
Shibuyaku
5728 5191
Open Mon–Sun 5–11pm
Shibuya station, east exit
[MAP p. 193 D4]

People who have spent their lives proclaiming that they hate tofu will eat their words at Tofu Cuisine Sorano. Dishes like the creamy, rich avocado tofu or crispy fried yuba (tofu skin) chips will likely convert the most die-hard tofu opponent. You'll find the restaurant on a narrow street alongside the train tracks. Head inside to its Zen-like interior and follow the pebble path past water features to one of the semi-private tatami rooms. It's fun to request the fresh tofu, which makes the journey from soy milk to tofu at your table. Most dishes come in around ¥1000, while the eclectic drinks list includes beverages for around ¥600 (be adventurous and try the delicious soy cocktail or the sake cocktail with apricot pieces). Tofu even extends to dessert; the tiramisu and cheesecake are wickedly good. And if you still stand by your tofu-loathing words, never fear: there's plenty here for meat-lovers too (the deep-fried black-bean chicken gets a thumbs-up from us).

12 ∫UZU CAFE

3F, Gems Building,
1-20-5 Jinnan, Shibuyaku
5428 3739
Open Sun–Thurs
11.30am–11pm, Fri–Sat
11.30am–11.30pm
Shibuya station, Hachiko exit
[MAP p. 192 C2]

This cosy third-floor cafe with a hotchpotch of vintage and modern industrial furniture is a quiet haven in the heart of busy Shibuya. Lunching shoppers and kids on dates are its main clientele, here to take advantage of the good-value lunch sets (available from 11.30am to 3pm). You can opt for either the special red rice or a pasta or salad dish; ask for the English menu. Curries and sandwiches cost even less and a beer will only tack around ¥300 onto your bill. Eleven different desserts will give you the energy you need to continue your retail odyssey. When you've shopped till you've dropped, you can pop back in the evening, when candlelight, an extensive cocktail menu and an all-you-can-drink deal provide the perfect conditions in which to unwind.

POCKET TIP

Sushi is fast, popular and delicious in Shibuya. Hunt out Umegaoka Sushi No Midori, Uobei or Genki.

13 ABOUT LIFE COFFEE

1-19-8 Dogenzaka, Shibuya
6809 0751
about-life.coffee
Open Mon–Fri 8.30am–
8.30pm, Sat–Sun 9am–7pm
Shibuya station, exit 1
[MAP p. 192 B3]

Just like the perfect espresso, this tiny, aromatic hole-in-the-wall cafe packs a flavourful punch, with the bonus of early opening hours. Owner Atsushi Sakao (from Onibus coffee) is Australian trained and architecturally savvy and uses beans from three of Tokyo's favourite coffee destinations: Switch, Onibus and Amameria. Choose from black (American or espresso), white (milk or soy) or filtered, quick brew and cold brew, they also offer an extra shot. Guest baristas and a small inner room that puts on regular shows by local and international illustrators and crafters make for the perfect blend. Grab a seat at a wooden bench. The sound of grinding beans and cheerful chatter between barista and customer drowns out the noise of Shibuya's streets. For a zero-waste coffee ask for a porcelain cup and then linger. The breakout crowd of Tokyoites and tourists gives this mini-coffee haven a festive atmosphere.

POCKET TIP

Coffee in Shibuya is a serious business. Head into Streamer, Bear Pond, Swing or Maruta Joy and Friends.

14 NONBEI YOKOCHO

Shibuya station, Hachiko exit
[MAP p. 193 D2]

Slip off the main drag in Shibuya to find Nonbei Yokocho, a shanty town of teeny-tiny bars squeezed into two beautiful lantern-lit alleyways. Some of the quaint little bars hold a total of only six people at a time. Others are spread over two floors, but even at these bigger places the most petite person will wonder if they'll be able to squeeze up the poky staircases. Drinking and stories are what you are here for and each bar has plenty of both. There's excellent food as well: everything from yakitori (grilled skewered meat) restaurants to home-style cooking, just like the salaryman's mother makes. Nonbei is slang for 'drunkard', so don't be shy – squash yourself into this delightful Tokyo time warp and get a few drinks into you.

POCKET TIP

Nearby Bic Camera is your one-stop electronics shop, with over five floors of cameras, drones, gadgets and accessories.

YOYOGI

The sprawling and beautiful Yoyogi Park is a cherry-blossom hot spot that served as a site for the Tokyo Olympics in 1964. Pockets of Yoyogi Park are more famous for the outrageously dressed Harajuku kids who like to hang out here and the old rock'n'rollers strutting their stuff.

Yoyogi precinct feels like it sprouted organically around the park, and has quickly become synonymous with Tokyo laid-back cool. This emerging neighbourhood feels a lot like Brooklyn or parts of Melbourne. It's all about books, coffee, small galleries and design and people gathering in cafes to chat about their latest zine or website project. The local charm makes it a wonderful place for a go-slow outing, so hire a bicycle and make a day of exploring this precinct.

→⊣ *Indie shopfront in Yoyogi*

SIGHTS
1. Yoyogi Park

SHOPPING
2. Rhythm and Books
3. Kio55

EATING & DRINKING
4. Little Nap Coffee Stand
5. Haritts
6. Fuglen

1 YOYOGI PARK

[MAP p. 194 A2]

A park of many moods, Yoyogi sits at the mid-point between Shibuya, Shinjuku, Harajuku and Yoyogi, a sizeable and impressive patch of green that pulses with the energy of its neighbours while providing the perfect, calm urban retreat. Opened in 1967 this mid-century park shows off its history proudly, showcasing **Yoyogi National Gymnasium** (*see* p. 27), stunning **Meiji Shrine** (*see* p. 26) and The Olympics Sample Garden, where participating countries brought cuttings of their national plants to create a 'garden of the world'. The Harajuku section plays host to Sunday jugglers, Elvis clones, bikers, karate practioners and the cosplay elite, whose adult version of dress-ups produces some impressive outfits. The 54 hectares are perfect for a morning jog or a picnic, especially during sakura (cherry blossom) season (grab picnic supplies from **Tokyu Food Show**, see p. 8). An avenue of zelkova trees, a cherry blossom grove, plum grove, a rose garden, ginkgo trees and even a bird sanctuary make it the perfect park and forest retreat. Festivals celebrating multiculturalism, rainbow pride, dog meet-ups and a famous antique market, all add to the vibrancy.

POCKET TIP

In the north-west part of Yoyogi Park you can hire bicycles from Tokyo Bike for a few hundred yen per hour.

2 RHYTHM AND BOOKƧ

1-9-15 Tomigaya, Shibuyaku
6407 0788
Open Mon–Fri 12pm–10pm,
Sat–Sun 12pm–8pm
Yoyogi-Koen station, exit 2
[MAP p. 199 C2]

Rhythm and Books is a tiny store jammed to the ceiling with retro books and music from Japan and Europe, all presided over by the dangling legs of a robot or two. You'll have to walk sideways like a crab to get through the skinny aisles, but the ramshackle collection of nostalgia here is artfully chosen and you're sure to unearth some real treasures. The postcards with hilarious hairstyles of '70s pop stars are a treat, but it's the great children's books, vintage Japanese magazines and novels with cool retro covers that make this place extra special.

3 KIO55

1-9-19 Tomigaya, Shibuyaku
6804 9888
Open Mon–Fri 11am–6pm,
Sat 12pm–6pm
Yoyogi-Koen station, exit 2
[MAP p. 199 C2]

Kio55 is a fantastic repository for the finest cooking and dining vessels; it stocks a beautiful range of kitchenware with a definite Scandinavian leaning. Designers are mostly unknown, which comes as a surprise given the fine quality of the bowls, plates, cutlery, carafes and enamelware on the shelves of the tiny, brightly lit store. Check out Tokyo designer Mutsumi's impressive wooden plate and bread knife, which somehow manages to be both traditional and futuristic at the same time. There's a selection of artfully arranged leather goods as well, including tote bags and purses. The entrance to the store is a little obscure, so keep your eyes peeled for the miniscule fish on a yellow board outside.

POCKET TIP
Yoyogi Park is home to a fantastic but irregular flea market. Check dates at yoyogikoen.info.

4 LITTLE NAP COFFEE STAND

5-65-4 Yoyogi, Shibuyaku
3466 0074
littlenap.jp
Open Tues–Sun 9am–7pm
Yoyogi-Hachiman station, exit 3
[MAP p. 199 C1]

Park your bicycle out the front of Little Nap and head into this coffee pit stop opposite **Yoyogi Park** (see p. 18). It's not so much a cafe as a hip shoebox, with Americana-style signage, big maps on the walls and bags of rustic charm. There are bags of coffee beans about the place too, as the owners roast their own. Seating is limited to a few stools inside and a bench outside, but no matter, as it's mostly about take-out here. The excellent drip coffee and espresso have made this the go-to place for anyone finding themselves in need of a pick-me-up after a picnic and a little nap in the park. While you're here, join the peeps taking happy snaps on the bench out the front.

POCKET TIP
If you are gluten free, head to Cafe Little Bird.

21

5 HARITT*s*

1-34-2 Uehara, Shibuyaku
3466 0600
Open Tues–Fri 8am–6pm,
Sat–Mon 11am–6pm
Yoyogi-Uehara station, exit 2
[MAP p. 199 A2]

Haritts is not that easy to find, so look for the cute little doughnut board that marks the tiny side street the shop is on. Behind the sliding door of this charming old Japanese house, the owners have perfected the art of the handmade doughnut. Get in early for sought-after flavours like cinnamon raisin or cream cheese, as these delicious, sugary dough clouds have a habit of running out quickly. In fact, to keep things fair, customers are limited to five doughnuts each on weekdays, three on weekends! Even the basic doughnuts here are lip-smackingly good, especially when downed with Haritts's coffee, and it's inexpensive too.

6 FUGLEN

1-6-11 Tomigaya, Shibuyaku
3481 0084
fuglen.no/japanese
Opening hours vary, see
website
Yoyogi-Koen station, exit 2
[MAP p. 199 C3]

This Norwegian coffee house is perfectly at home in Yoyogi. Its interior is warm and inviting, with a '50s-slash-'60s modernist Japanese bent, and quality siphon coffee is served, making it a great place to start your day or relax on a lazy afternoon. Expect the benches to be propping up blonde models and Scandiphiles, but locals also flock here to unwind. Warm-wood shelves display ceramic pieces from top Scandinavian designers like Stig Lindberg and Lisa Larson and it's all for sale! At night Fuglen spills onto the street and morphs into an ultra-hip bar selling Norwegian and Japanese craft beers, and some very tempting cocktails.

POCKET TIP

Yoyogi has four train stations; Yoyogi Uehara, Yoyogi Koen, Yoyogi Hachiman and Yoyogi.

HARAJUKU

Buzzing Harajuku has been reinventing itself as a youth destination since the 1920s. From the mad crush of pedestrian-only Takeshita Dori to the majestic sweep of Omotesando, a wide, tree-lined street reminiscent of a French boulevard, this is where young Tokyoites come to flaunt eye-popping fashion and queue for the newest cafe.

Omotesando is the epicentre of Harajuku. International brands vie for attention here, showcasing beautifully curated fashion in spectacular buildings created by a who's who of Japanese architects. Boasting a network of seriously fabulous backstreets, Harajuku holds the key to some of Tokyo's unmissable shopping and dining experiences.

↤ *Family attending a wedding at Meiji Shrine*

1 MEIJI JINGŪ (MEIJI ∫HRINE)

1-1 Yoyogikamizonocho, Shibuya
3379 5511
meijijingu.or.jp
Opening hours vary
Harajuku station or Meiji-
Jingumae station, exit 2
[MAP p. 194 A1]

The contrast between the city and the serene, whispering glades of the Meiji Shinto Shrine couldn't be more acute. Head out of busy Harajuku station and turn towards the towering Tori gate. You'll pass through deep woods, see sake barrels for the gods and small spiritual tori gates and statues. The sunshine never hits the ground here, filtered gently through the tall cedars, and it is serene and deeply atmospheric as you stroll toward the expansive shrine, a relic of old Tokyo, still thriving in modern times. The path is known as a shrine forest, dense with chinquapin, oak and camphor trees amongst its 350 varieties, all planted as an 'eternal' forest, rejuvenating itself. When Emperor Meiji died in 1912, he was deified in the shrine, made to immortalise his earthly soul. It was rebuilt after the original was bombed in World War Two but remains ancient, proud and impressive. If you're lucky, you might also get to see a spectacular Shinto wedding ceremony on the grounds.

2 YOYOGI NATIONAL GYMNAJIUM

2-1, Jinnan, Shibuya
3468 1171
jpnsport.go.jp/yoyogi
Harajuku station,
Omotosandoguchi exit
[MAP p. 194 A3]

POCKET TIP
Make sure you walk around the whole building. It's great from every angle.

A short walk from bustling Harajuku, the Yoyogi National Gymnasium is a modernist marvel perched on the edge of **Yoyogi Park** (*see* p. 18). Superstar architect Kenzo Tange designed the building for the 1964 Olympics, which saw Tokyo emerge from a dark post-war period and showcase to the world a powerful vision of development and inclusion. The building reflects the tension, flow and agility of athletes. You can see how it shaped many of the stadiums that came after it – the curved lines, tensile steel 'circus ropes' and the vast surrounding spaces. Despite being over 50 years old, the building won't be out of place when it serves as an arena for the handball at Tokyo's 2020 Olympic Games. Spectacular and commanding, it's just a stone's throw from the verdant paths that lead to the **Meiji Shrine** (*see* p. 26), making it the perfect architectural conversation between the spiritual aesthetic of the modern and the ancient.

3 KIDDY LAND

6-1-9 Jingumae, Shibuyaku
3409 3431
kiddyland.co.jp
Open Mon–Fri 11am–9pm,
Sat–Sun 10.30am–9pm
Harajuku station, Omotesando
exit, or Meiji-Jingumae station,
exit 4
[MAP p. 194 C3]

Kiddy Land is one of Tokyo's quintessential shopping experiences. It's a toy store like no other. Kids and kidults flock here for new fads and old favourites among the constantly evolving selections. Searching for limited-edition figurines? You'll get them here. Need a kimono for your Blythe fashion doll? No problem. Hello Kitty and Miffy obsessive? Sure thing! Star Wars headphones, character lunch boxes, crazy phone accessories: it's all here jam-packed into five mesmerising floors. Some of the store's best items can be nabbed for next to nothing, but the serious collector can go to town here as well. Its motto 'For the human smile' sums up how you will feel as you walk out of Kiddy Land with your stash.

POCKET TIP

Head to Playmountain for a clever mix of interior wares by contemporary and local designers.

4 BIG LOVE RECORDS

3F, 2-31-3 Jingumae, Shibuyaku
5775 1315
bigloverecords.jp
Open Mon 3–8pm, Tues–Sun 1–10pm
Meiji-Jingumae station, exit 5
[MAP p. 195 A1]

You have to go to the edge of Harajuku, down a random side street and up several flights of stairs to find Big Love Records, but it's oh-so worth it. This would have to be one of the coolest record stores/cafes/bars in the world. It's amazing what they pack into the small space here, with racks of great music squeezed between a bar that looks like a Mexican cantina and a tiny rustic cafe. The vinyl, zines and cassette tapes will take you back to the glory days of the '80s, but there are plenty of up-to-date international indie releases as well. The independent ethos extends to the bar's rotating crop of rare Japanese craft beers, which you can gulp down while listening to some truly select tunes.

5 GALERIE DOUX DIMANCHE

3-5-6 Jingumae, Shibuyaku
3408 5120
2dimanche.com
Open Mon–Sun 12pm–7.30pm
Omotesando station, exit A2
[MAP p. 195 B2]

It's easy to see owner Hisashi Tokuyoshi's love of all things French and Scandinavian in this craft oasis in a cosy backstreet, just minutes from Harajuku's chaotic core. Make no mistake though: Galerie Doux Dimanche is thoroughly Japanese in its aesthetic. The delightfully twee interior is a mini gallery with a handicraft store attached. Always turning the cute factor up to 11, the gallery shows works by local illustrators and artists, while the store has a colourful selection of French-style bric-a-brac, fabric, stationery and charming stuff to style up your home. In addition to the gallery and shop, the publisher **Paumes** is located upstairs. It produces small inspirational books and zines that explore the environments of creative people globally, and curates the exhibitions for the gallery downstairs.

POCKET TIP
Look out for gorgeous cards and prints by Tokyo artist Yumi Kitagishi.

6 MINTDE/IGN/

5-49-5 Jingumae, Shibuya
6427 9906
mint-designs.com
Open Mon–Sun 11am–8pm
Omotesando station, exit B2
[MAP p. 195 A4]

Hokuto Katsui and Nao Yagi
started Mintdesigns in 2001
with a view to presenting
new and fresh women's
fashion designs (hence the
name). The style is breezy,
light and stylish – Japanese
shapes, colour clashes, fabric
and pattern mash-ups show
that Mintdesigns draws
from a Japanese aesthetic
to make pieces look young
and contemporary. Clothes
are quirky, with a sense of
fun, but always wearable in
the everyday. The store is
beautiful, a concrete bunker full
of bright pops of colour where
the clothes look like they are
hanging magically from the
ceiling. Accessories, socks,
tights and scarves all add
extra allure. Recipients of the
prestigious Moët et Chandon
New Designers Award in 2005,
they have three stores to date
and participated in shows and
exhibitions across Japan and
the world. Katsui and Yagi
are believers in serendipity.
A major part of their philosophy
rests on the 'happy accident'
occurring in their designs.
As they say, 'failures are
more thrilling than what we
originally envisioned.'

POCKET TIP
The wonderful
gallery at the top
of the Louis Vuitton
building is free.

mint des i g n s

31

7 HAGURUMA

4-5-4 Jingumae, Shibuyaku
150 0001
Open Wed–Mon 11am–8pm
Omotesando station, exit A2
[MAP p. 195 B3]

Are you passionate about pen and ink? Are you into sending messages the old way and want to give your missives the personal touch? Head to Haguruma (admire the always inspiring window display), and roll out one of their sizeable drawers to see what paper treasures are inside. A third-generation family business, they have quietly been revolutionising the art and craft of stationery. Shelves of cards, boxes, note paper, ribbons and other embellishments give letter writers plenty of choice. The beautiful letterpress, bespoke invites and cards come in a surprising array of shapes and colours. Designs ranging from animals and flowers to traditional shapes and symbols all use paper of the highest craftsmanship. We love the #700 card range with animal and fruit motifs – revered symbols of luck, prosperity, legend or beauty. Make sure to pick up one of their business cards that converts into a tiny envelope.

8 TORAYA AN STAND

3-12-16 Kita Aoyama, Minato
6450 6720
Open Mon–Sun 11am–7pm
Omotesando station, exit B2
[MAP p. 195 A4]

Toraya is one of Japan's oldest and most revered makers of 'an wagashi', a traditional Japanese sweet made from adzuki (red) bean paste. For over 500 years their exquisite sweets, shapes, designs and packaging have been the pinnacle of beauty, held up as the country's finest. The An Stand blends the old with the new, the Japanese and western. The red bean paste is still the key ingredient, updated to blend with a mix of western desserts and drinks and in Japanese favourites. Try the unique red bean paste latte, a coffee with bean paste stirred into it. Other surprises include red bean paste on toast, a giant cookie and a bread-style éclair where the red bean paste complements a cream cheese filling. The store is a minimal architectural two-storey treasure. Sip your red bean coffee sitting on a stone sculpture out the front, downstairs at the communal table or share your sweets upstairs with the cute Toraya tiger prowling in the corner.

POCKET TIP
The streets around Toraya are full of interesting small shops and cafes.

TORAYA CAFÉ · AN STAND

9 KOFFEE MAMEYA

4-15-3 Jingumae, Shibuya
koffee-mameya.com
Open Mon–Sun 10am–6pm
Omotesando station, exit A2
[MAP p. 195 A2]

Step through the black box and onto the stone path, turn right at the tortured tree and enter a world of aromas, beans, pouring, grinding, syphoning, filtering and savouring. Owner of legendary Omotesando Koffee, which closed down in 2015, Eiichi Kunitomo has set up shop in the same spot, and it's still a tiny haven for caffeine obsessives. Mameya translates as 'bean shop' and the barista is king – they'll build up your coffee profile until the perfect brew is at your fingertips. The size of the architectural blonde wood room with its wall of coffee beans makes for the perfect take-out coffee hit and run. The coffee is extracted from the world's very best beans and brewed with a pour-over or an espresso machine. It's almost a mini laboratory – find your favourite bean from the varietals on offer (a taste test is best), have them packed into Mameya's gorgeous little coffee bags and then take them home to re-create your own. Ask about their coffee lessons and workshops.

10 MAISEN

4-8-5 Jingumae, Shibuyaku
3470 0071
Open Mon–Sun 11am–10pm
Omotesando station, exit A2
[MAP p. 195 A2]

To say Maisen is a Tokyo institution is a bit of an understatement. Legions of loyal followers, both local and international, make their way through Harajuku's winding backstreets to this famous joint to order the tonkatsu (delicate pork in breadcrumbs). Join the queue (which can be long but moves quickly) and ask to be seated in the beautiful former bathhouse or the delightful traditional tatami (Japanese floor mat) room. Dishes range from excellent to awesome. The pinnacle of the menu is the black pork; smother it in one of Maisen's two signature 'secret' sauces (we prefer the thick, sweet plum one), then eat it with mounds of addictive shredded cabbage. One of the well-chosen sakes is the perfect way to wash it down. If you don't eat pork, there are also delicious prawn, salad and sashimi options. On your way out, make sure you buy some secret sauce to wow your friends back home.

AOYAMA

South of the thoroughfare of Aoyama Dori, the
madness of Harajuku and Omotesando gives way to
chic, understated Tokyo style in Aoyama. There is an
atmosphere of calm in these leafy streets lined with
fashion boutiques, florists, organic cafes and stores
selling beautiful handmade wares.

In-the-know international and local shoppers come
here to update their wardrobes. Issey Miyake and
Comme des Garçons command much of the real
estate here, and statues, art projects and installations
make the stores look more like galleries than retail
outlets. Coveted Japanese and European fashion
labels are housed in famous architectural buildings,
brave new additions to the landscape of reflective
temples, shrines and samurai houses.

→ *Entrance to the Nezu Museum*

1 NEZU MUSEUM

6-5-1 Minami Aoyama, Minato
3400 2536
nezu-muse.or.jp
Open Mon–Sun 10am–5pm
Omotesando station, exit A5
[MAP p. 195 C4]

Philanthropist, politician and president of the Tobu Railway Company, Kaichiro Nezu was an avid practitioner of the tea ceremony and a collector of pre-modern Japanese and East Asian art. His son established a gallery and a garden to celebrate both. The original was built on the grounds of the Nezu family residence in 1940–41; architect Kengo Kuma later reconstructed the museum after World War Two fires. A striking minimalist space is made warm by bamboo walkways and low-mood lighting. Lovers of calligraphy, scrolls, paintings and textiles will be entranced by the collection. The 18th-century Emperor and Empress dolls, 17th-century Kosode (silk robes) and Buddha statues dating back to the 3rd and 6th centuries, are just some of the standouts. The gardens host tea ceremonies in tiny huts secluded among the foliage. Look out for women in traditional kimono often seen taking tea. A contemporary cafe serves lunch and cake sets, and the garden's silhouetted shapes are lit on to the canvas sail walls.

POCKET TIP
Higashiya Man is a hole-in-the-wall sweet shop that specialies in high-end manju (steamed bun sweets) and other delights. Their seasonal creations are stunning and sell out in hours.

2 WATARIUM

3-7-6 Jingumae, Shibuya
3402 3001
watarium.co.jp
Open Wed–Mon 11am–9pm
Gaiemmae station, exit 3
[MAP p. 195 B1]

Housing a revolving collection of Tokyo's most avant-garde art shows, this metallic sliver of a building – a looming wedge of machine parts and shining surfaces with well-tooled grooves – was constructed by Mario Botta in 1990. Several small floors around a central well see artworks spread over nooks and crannies, along corridor walls and suspended from ceilings. At any given time you could be looking at recent graduate works or the latest local, national and international art mavericks. While viewing artworks, you might also be staring down onto an impromptu band squeezing abstract sounds out of reconstructed electronica or instruments modified beyond their original purpose. Past exhibitions include Ryuchi Sakamoto's aural sculpture 'async,' and the 'reborn' recycled art festival. The ground floor gallery shop has a fantastic selection of art books and stationery, and art lectures and events are held regularly.

POCKET TIP

For anyone who still has a paper diary or keeps losing digital passwords, head into Tobichi for the world's coolest personal planner, the Hobonichi Techo.

3 IMABARI TOWEL

2F, 203, 5-3-10 Minami-
Aoyama, Minato-ku
6427 2941
imabaritowel-minamiaoyama.jp
Open Fri–Tues 11am–7.30pm
Omotesando station, exit B1
[MAP p. 195 C4]

Get 'knuckle deep' into
the fluffiness of the towels,
facecloths, socks and dressing
gowns here, all made from
cotton or bamboo blended
with the 'soft water' of the
Shikoku region. The store has
beautiful, blonde wood shelves
stacked with colour-coded
and pattern-coded towels. It's
artfully arranged and makes
you wish you could get your
bathroom redesigned just
like it. If you feel your towel
knowledge is lacking, check
the website and sign up to
become a towel sommelier.
Learn all about different towels,
and uses of towels, and how
to find a towel to properly fit
yours – or somebody else's –
needs. Your excessive towel
knowledge will be a hit at
dinner parties and any other
random social engagement.

POCKET TIP
Aoyama's side streets
are a showcase for
some of Tokyo's
most interesting
architecture.

4 UT∫UWA KAEDE

3-5-5 Minami Aoyama, Minato
3402 8110
utsuwa-kaede.com
Open Wed–Mon 12pm–9pm
Omotesando station, exit A4
[MAP p. 195 C3]

Japanese pottery and ceramics are among the most exquisite in the world and at Utsuwa Kaede the beauty of the seasons is woven into the integral fabric of these pieces. Elements are given form – wood, glass, earth and light filter into the homewares, and small imperfections make the pieces special and unique. Delicate and personal, Kaede's pottery makes the most immaculate gift or keepsake. The only problem you might have is not wanting to use the cups, teapots and plates, preferring to display them. Daily use seems too normal, regular, commonplace for such beauty. The small space diffuses with outside light, and all manner of beautiful and resplendent objects are arranged against shelves making the room appear more like an exquisite gallery space than a store.

5 COMME DES GARÇONS

5-2-1 Minami-Aoyama,
Minato-ku
3406 3951
comme-des-garcons.com
Open Mon–Sun 11am–8pm
Omotesando station, exit A5
[MAP p. 195 B4]

This flagship store for Comme des Garçons is a showroom that blurs the lines between art and retail. Designer Rei Kawakubo is the founder of the store and her tortured futurist kimonos and Gothic lace party dresses make the space feel more like a contemporary art exhibition than a fashion store. High-flyers with a taste for the edgy head here to see if they can carry off Kawakubo's intricately engineered creations. They'll never look as good as the staff though, who float around the store like museum exhibits on a catwalk. If your budget doesn't stretch to a Comme des Garçons dress or jacket, you can always pick up one of its beautiful Japan-only fragrances or ubercool T-shirts.

6 PALACE AOYAMA

Palace Aoyama, 6-1-6
Minami-Aoyama, Minato
3499 7605
arts-science.com
Open Mon–Sun 12pm–8pm
Omotesando station, exit A5
[MAP p. 195 C4]

Spend an afternoon in the beautifully curated fashion and accessory stores in this '70s apartment block. The array of makers here give this corner of Aoyama its own special allure. **Arts & Science**, creators of beautiful and edgy clothing and shoes that play by their own rules, have a main store and a number of shops here. Creator Sonya Park's brand has a considered aesthetic and a loyal following of Tokyoites and internationals. **&Shop** sells genderless clothing and accessories. It also acts as a conduit for experimental exhibitions and co-labs, so whenever you visit something innovative will be happening. **At the Corner** is a stunning, dark and minimalist design shop with an exceptional range of experimental clothing and luxurious homewares. Sister store **Shoes & Things** uses Japanese leather to craft the most immaculate footwear for men and women. **Higashi** showcases the finest examples of handmade Japanese homewares, including ceramics, teapots and cutlery. You'll wish you'd packed an extra suitcase.

POCKET TIP
Check out the mini bespoke stores in the Aoyama Heights building.

43

7 SPIRAL DESIGN MARKET

5-6-23 Minami-Aoyama,
Minato
3498 1171
spiral.co.jp
Open Mon–Sun 11am–8pm
Omotesando station, exit B1
[MAP p. 195 A4]

Spiral Design Market is a design store, cafe, bar and gallery rolled into one. The snail-shell-shaped ramp that gives Spiral its name winds through a gallery space showing special exhibitions by emerging designers, architects, furniture makers, jewellers and artists. On the second floor you'll find a skillfully curated selection of homewares, which the store markets as 'simple products for everyday use'. The beautiful range is well priced, so you're sure to find something to style up your home.

POCKET TIP

Spiral Design Market, Sakurai and the Minä Perhonen's Call store are all housed in the same building.

8 SAKURAI JAPANESE TEA EXPERIENCE

Spiral building, 5-6-23 Minami Aoyama, Minato
3571 1551
sakurai-tea.jp
Open Mon–Sun 11am–8pm
Omotesando station, exit B1
[MAP p. 195 A4]

After 14 years perfecting his craft, Tea Master Shinya Sakurai opened his contemporary tea-house – a modern version of the ancient ceremony. On the refurbished fifth floor of the Spiral building, it's a wonderful date venue or place to take design friends. You'll be shown to a counter seat, by a square bench, where the tea master works his magic for all to see, whisking, agitating and pouring – tea making that commands silence. A minimalist space is accented by brass and polished concrete. The glass sink is a feature, a waterfall disappearing into its shallow shimmering bowl. Tea is roasted in-store and seasonal varieties are brewed using elaborate kettles and teapots and poured into beautiful ceramics. Enjoy your tea with some of Tokyo's prettiest seasonal wagashi (traditional Japanese sweets), while you gaze out over the impressive skyline.

9 A TO Z CAFE

5F, 5-8-3 Minami-Aoyama,
Minato
5464 0281
Open Mon–Sun
11.30am–11.30pm
Omotesando station, exit B1
[MAP p. 195 B4]

The centrepiece of this whimsical fifth floor cafe is an amazing wooden house, a permanent art installation that's a reconstruction of pop artist Yoshitomo Nara's studio. Mastering the art of kawaii – that cute quality that pervades Japanese culture – Nara's paintings of impish, wide-eyed moppets line the walls in this cafe, peering out of intimate recesses and nooks, seemingly watching you as you eat. The rest of the cafe is all painted pipes and wooden beams combined with a mashup of found furniture. Between 11.30am and 2pm, the set lunch is a steal. Otherwise join the crowd of bohemian locals, art students and couples and mooch away the afternoon sipping coffee and grazing on the house speciality of pumpkin coconut cream cake. If you can't get a table near the wooden house, get one next to the window for a fantastic view over the rooftops of Aoyama. At night, the mood shifts as a DJ hits the decks and coffee moves over for cocktails.

10 AOYAMA FLOWER MARKET TEA HOUƧE

5-1-2 Minami-Aoyama, Minato
3400 0087
Open Mon–Sun 11am–6.30pm
Omotesando station, exit A5
[MAP p. 195 B3]

As you enter this secret garden hidden behind the Aoyama Flower Market, the scent of flowers wafts overhead. Inside the beautiful teahouse, intricate lights entwine with dangling blooms and glass-topped tables reveal vines that curl around your feet. Take a seat and choose from a wide range of specialist tea blends and herbal teas, perhaps channelling your inner quaintness with an Earl Grey accompanied by scones and cream. Dainty little cakes are also on the menu, as is French toast, but our pick is the 'flower parfait', a muddle of rose jelly, ice-cream and mousse studded with fresh flowers. Grab a bouquet or one of the teahouse's signature blends on your way out and take some of this little patch of heaven with you.

ROPPONGI

Roppongi has long held the crown as the go-to precinct to party all night and catch the last train home. Chaotic and noisy, it has looming overpasses and streets so wide you can't see the other side. While its seedy reputation has been hard earned and is well deserved, the precinct has undergone a cultural renaissance over the last ten years with the emergence of an 'art triangle', featuring some of the world's finest galleries and architecture.

Azabu-Juban is right next door, but it's more sedate, with a village-like atmosphere, cobbled streets, traditional shops and family businesses which are in stark contrast to party-central Roppongi.

→ Mori Gardens, Roppongi Hills

1 ART TRIANGLE

Roppongi station, various exits
[MAP p. 196 B1]

With the completion of the
National Art Center, the
Suntory Museum of Art,
and the already established
Mori Art Museum, the
once slightly sleazy Roppongi
suddenly found itself with
some of Tokyo's, and the
world's, most incredible art
spaces. Further accented
by the **21_21 Design Site**,
the **Fujifilm Square** and
Midtown's Design Hub,
it's a premium, family friendly
destination. The numerous
galleries are within walking
distance from each other and
visiting any time is unmissable.
The National Art Center is a
majestic embankment of glass
and steel housing ten galleries
over three floors that play host
to constantly changing national
and international contemporary
and traditional exhibitions.
The Suntory Museum of
Art shows Japanese art
and craft including Noren,
Kimono, Ukiyo E and other
representations of a creative
flourishing throughout Japan's
history, in a series of revolving
exhibitions. Mori Art Museum,
a sky-piercing tower with 54
floors, is devoted to national
and international contemporary
art. You'll see memorable
exhibitions and a distracting
view of an extraordinary
urban sprawl.

POCKET TIP
Each gallery has a
great shop.

2 UGUISU THE LITTLE SHOPPE

Room 7, 3-3-23 Azabudai, Minato
6426 5949
uguisulittleshoppe.com
Opening hours vary, check website
Roppongi station, exit 3
[MAP p. 197 D3]

Tucked away in a quiet lane just a ten-minute stroll from the madness of Roppongi station is a charming 1930's building housing the perfect craft and homewares store. Owner Hiki has curated a beautiful and playful collection of must-have and hard-to-find items from Japanese and international makers. Linen, jewellery, tableware and stationery are crafted with love by passionate, individual makers. You'll adore the contemporary takes on Japanese classics like furoshiki (wrapping cloths), Japanese traditional candles (handmade and vegan), the Yuikoubou label's natural indigo-dyed earnings and Haibara Japanese Stationery, but there's plenty more to love. If you can't fit everything in your suitcase, they ship worldwide and you can even keep shopping on their online store once you get home.

3 TOKYO MIDTOWN

9-7-1 Akasaka, Minato
3475 3100
tokyo-midtown.com/en
Open Mon–Sun 11am–9pm
Roppongi station, exit 8
[MAP p. 196 C1]

Midtown is a contemporary shopping centre surrounded by greenery, sculpture and the wonderful **21_21 Design Site**. The building houses the **Suntory Museum of Art** (*see* p. 50) and some excellent shopping. Highlights on the first (ground) floor include an exquisite **Toraya** confectionery store, with a gallery showcasing the history of wagashi (Japanese sweets) and a cafe. **Nakagawa Masashichi Shotengai** is a gift shop specialising in updates on traditional items. Lunch at **Suzunami**, a popular fish-based eatery, or buy some sashimi at **Preece** supermarket and have a picnic. Pop into **Sadoharu Aoki** for Japanese fusion sweet delights including the unforgettable macha éclair. **Dashi Chazuke-en dashi** has dashi (a tasty fish- and seaweed-based stock) in amazing packaging. On the third floor, **Nihonbashi Kiya**, founded in 1792, is a gallery-like space that sells exquisite knives, cutlery and cookware. Excellent hand-crafted homewares can be found at **Wise-Wise** and **The Cover Nippon**.

4 SHIROIKURO

2-8-1 Azabu-Juban, Minato
3454 7225
Open Mon–Sun 10am–6pm
Azabu-Juban station, exit 1
[MAP p.196 C4]

Walk the quiet Azabu-Juban backstreets towards Roppongi and you'll come across this tiny local dessert store. It has carved out a name for itself as the go-to place for sweets, ice-cream and cake. A white cat will usher you in to the modern rework of an old Japanese house. Meaning 'black and white', Shiroikuro's name is fitting: many of its delicacies have a sweet white exterior that hides a dense, delicious black soybean centre. The most eye-catching dessert is probably the Swiss roll, but the popular choice is the salted mocha dumpling. Go on: see if you can eat just the one.

POCKET TIP
Naniwaya Sohonten in Azabu Juban dates back to 1909. It is one of Tokyo's best Taiyaki (sweet fish-shaped pastry) shops.

5 GOGYO

1-4-36 Nishi-Azabu, Minato
5775 5566
Open Mon–Sat 11.30am–3am,
Sun 11.30am–12am
Roppongi station, exit 1C
[MAP p. 196 A2]

Gogyo is an institution in Kyoto, a ramen (noodle soup) joint set in a stunning old building with a great story to tell. While this Roppongi branch doesn't have an interesting story or particularly spectacular surrounds, it does have the same delicious ramen (ask for the English menu). Years of experience have gone into perfecting its version of the Japanese staple, so expect perfectly cooked noodles, more-ish soup and ever-so-tender slices of pork. Our pick is the unforgettable burnt-miso ramen, a dark, rich broth with lip-burning oil floating on top. Its deep smoky flavour makes it irresistible, and it's also perfect after a late-night drinking session to soak up that one too many.

6 UDON KUROSAWA

6-11-16 Roppongi, Minato-ku
3403 9638
Open Mon–Fri 11.30am–3pm
& 5–11pm, Sat–Sun
11.30am–11pm
Azabu-Juban station, exit 4
[MAP p. 196 C3]

This small, rustic restaurant specialises in the lighter Kyoto-style udon noodle. While all the dishes are excellent, locals come for the delicious curry nanban, an udon dish with a dashi stock. Our pick, though, is the fresh seasonal udon. Udon Kurosawa is particularly good at night, when it broadens the food menu to include izakaya classics. Ask to try delicious regional sakes, delivered in handmade ceramics. There's a rumour that this place is owned by famous film director Akira Kurosawa's son. Judging by the restaurant's attention to detail and excellent standards, we wouldn't be surprised if it's true.

7 TOFU UKAI

4-4-13 Shiba-Koen, Minato-ku
3436 1028
ukai.co.jp
Open Mon–Sun 11am–10pm
Akabanebashi station
[MAP p. 197 F4]

Under the watchful eye of Tokyo Tower you'll find this stunning tofu-specialist restaurant cocooned in a beautiful garden. Set in a Samurai-era merchant's house that contains one of Japan's oldest sake mills, Ukai is a labyrinth of 55 intimate rooms, all sparsely furnished with tatami floor mats. Each of the rooms overlooks lush grounds, the thatched roof of the grill hut, koi (fish) ponds and even a waterwheel. The food here is amazing: delectable, seasonal kaiseki cuisine (a traditional, multi-course Japanese meal), augmented by the impossibly fresh tofu. Weekend lunch sets cost around ¥5500 to ¥6800, while dinner will set you back anywhere between ¥87,000 and ¥129,000. While Ukai might not make it onto a cheap-eats list, it will undoubtedly make it onto your list of unforgettable Tokyo dining experiences.

POCKET TIP

Despite the Skytree's (see p. 92) popularity, Tokyo Tower remains the sentimental favourite and boasts impressive views.

GINZA

Built on a swamp and burnt almost to the ground in 1872, this opulent precinct has risen like a phoenix from the ashes. This is Tokyo at its grandest. Home to some of the world's oldest and most luxurious department stores, it's the best place to glimpse kimono-clad women shopping in fashion boutiques and lunching in Michelin-starred restaurants.

Classic Japanese paper, fabric and incense shops and established tempura houses are dotted among the big flagship stores and luxe European brands (check out the eye-popping Louis Vuitton building). Don't mind the iconic Wako Clock keeping time; instead, stick around as day turns to night to see one of Tokyo's quintessential neon landscapes.

→ *Packaged wagashi at Mitsukoshi department store*

1 TOYOSU MARKET

6-4-12 Toyosu, Koto-Ku
toyosumarketevent.jp/
Shijo-mae station
[MAP p. 191 F3]

2018 saw the opening of the successor to iconic Tsukiji Fish Market, the bright and shiny modern structure known as Toyosu Market. Tokyo legend Tsukiji was a market like no other, one of the world's biggest and most famous, where auctions took place almost daily and most of Tokyo's seafood intake was sourced, sorted and bid for in a flurry of (very) early morning activity. Two kilometres away, Toyosu's corridors are crammed with containers brimming with all manner of marine life from the recognisable to the possible evolutionary stages of life forms. The squeamish should probably stay on the sidelines and just partake of the fish and octopods when they have safely become sushi or sashimi in one of the area's eateries. A gallery allows people to observe auctions taking place, something that had been off limits to the public for years at Tsukiji. For the nostalgic, Tsukiji's outer market remains – we will still wander the ramshackle alleyways for the authentic atmosphere and great seafood.

POCKET TIP

The Okuno Building and the Ginza Graphic gallery are two of our favourite places to see art in Tokyo.

2 NAT/UNO

6-7-4 Ginza, Chuo-ku
3569 0952
Open Mon–Sat 10am–8pm,
Sun 10am–7pm
Ginza station, exit A2
[MAP p. 204 B3]

The Japanese take their
chopsticks seriously; it's not
uncommon for them to have
their own personalised set.
This is where Natsuno comes
in. Like an Ollivander's Wand
Shop of chopsticks, there are
over 2500 varieties made from
bamboo, lacquer and wood,
all stacked high up the walls.
The colourful store also stocks
hashioki (chopstick rests),
kokeshi (handmade wooden
folk-art dolls) and a hotchpotch
of traditional souvenirs, but
it's definitely the chopsticks
you're here for. Prices range
from around ¥300 for the simple
designs right up to ¥100,000
for the serious chopstick
connoisseur. Could these
top-end ones have a phoenix
feather or essence of unicorn
in them?

3 LOFT

3F-6F, 2-4-6 Ginza, Chuo
3562 6210
loft.co.jp/lp/ginzaloft
Open Mon–Sun 11am–9pm
Ginza station, exit 4
[MAP p. 204 B3]

Loft is the kind of household goods store that dreams are made of and it's still where we go to see how well Tokyo does retail. It's a colourful selection of contemporary and functional homewares, stationery and lifestyle products that will have you browsing for hours and mentally revamping rooms in your house for days. You'll find everything – the latest trends in skincare and make-up, coffee pots and ceramics, brightly coloured lunch-box sets or even smiley face sponges made of high-tech materials. Stationery fans will be in heaven, with a wall of MT washi (paper tape) and a 'Pencil Bar', with the most amazing selection you'll come across. The pour-over coffee pots, filters and cups are a real standout, and the tea range is just as covetable – perfect for gifts to take home (or for yourself). If you're in Tokyo for Christmas, Halloween or Valentine's Day, there'll be catchy jingles and killer displays. For 30 years Loft's reputation as a must-visit store has not faltered.

POCKET TIP

Some of Tokyo's best art can be found in Ginza's skincare and make-up stores. The Shiseido Gallery, and the Pola Museum of Art both hold world-class exhibitions.

4 GINZA ITOYA

2-7-15 Ginza, Chuo-ku
3561 8311
Open Mon–Sat 10am–8pm,
Sun 10am–7pm
Ginza station, exit A13
[MAP p. 204 B3]

Ginza Itoya was founded in 1904 but it's definitely not stuck in its ways. Its mash-up of traditional and contemporary has made it a popular destination for anyone wanting to get in on Tokyo's stationery obsession. Over twelve bustling floors you'll find calligraphy tools next to high-tech pens, paper products of all shapes and sizes, beautiful origami paper, fans, fabric, cards, washi (paper tape) and glue, all artfully chosen. Check out its range of bags too, perfect for your iPad and laptop. The giant red paperclip sign says it all: look up to see it protruding from the building like a piece of modern art.

5 AKOMEYA

2-2-6 Ginza, Chuo-ku
6758 0270
Open Mon–Sun 11am–9pm
(shop); 11.30am–10pm
(cafe and bar)
Ginza station, exit A2
[MAP p. 204 B2]

If you have a hankering for
rice, it's safe to say that
Akomeya will have what you
want. It sells over 6000 items
relating in some way to
the great Japanese staple.
Downstairs, supermarket
aisles are loaded with sake,
seasonings, rice desserts and
more, while upstairs there's
great kitchenware and utensils
to eat rice with. The grain
selections come from all over
Japan, and you can even get
your rice polished to go. In-
shop cafe **Akomeya Chubo**
has delicious rice-based,
health-conscious dishes, while
Akomeya Bar at the front of
the store is great for a good stiff
drink – a rice cocktail, perhaps?

POCKET TIP

Ginza is a wonderful
precinct to shop for
Kimono. We love to
visit Ginza Kimono
Aoki, Antique Mall
and Echigoya.

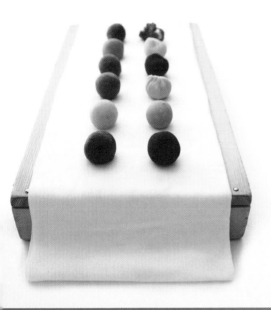

6 HIGAﾉHIYA

2F, Pola Ginza Building,
1-7-7 Ginza, Chuo-ku
3538 3230
higashiya.com
Open Mon–Sun 11am–3pm &
5–9pm
Ginza station, exit A13
[MAP p. 204 B2]

It'd be easy enough to walk
straight past the Pola building
if you didn't know what
treasures lay within, but then
you'd miss out on luxurious
teahouse Higashiya. The
interior is classic Japanese
with a minimal contemporary
makeover. Choose a bench
seat or sit at a table and watch
as the staff pour hot water
from giant copper kettles into
bowls and then whisk in green
tea. Delectable lunch sets are
served on equally delectable
ceramics, or you can opt for
afternoon tea and sweets.
There are over 30 varieties
of tea to try, all perfect when
accompanied by delicate
Japanese mochi (sweet rice
cakes), which are arranged in
boxes like little gems. If you're
short on time, the small shop at
the entrance sells Higashiya's
tea, sweets and elegant
homewares to take away.

7 GINZA SUSHI AOKI

2F, 6-7-4 Ginza, Chuo-ku
3289 1044
sushiaoki.jp
Open Mon–Sun 12pm–2pm &
5–10pm
Ginza station, exit A2
[MAP p. 204 B3]

One of the most respected
(and expensive) sushi
restaurants in Tokyo, Aoki
prides itself on the freshest
fish served at the perfect
temperature. This is no sushi
conveyor belt. Most people in
the tiny room sit at the counter
and watch the master chefs do
their thing, expertly carving
gleaming fish and laying it on
pillows of hand-rolled sushi
rice. Request the omakase
(chef's choice) if you want
one of the chefs to psychically
know what you want. Our
hesitation towards the sea
urchin was met with a gentle
coaxing – our chef knew we
would like it, and we did! Did
we mention that Aoki has a
Michelin star? Make sure you
order the lunch or dinner sets
though, which are inexpensive.

POCKET TIP
The charming Kissaten
Café L'Ambre will transport
you back to the mid-20th
century. Make sure to try
the coffee jelly.

POCKET TIP

Kimuraya Bakery was established in 1874 and is famous for its excellent Melonpan and Sakadane Sakura, a salty bread with a sweet filling.

8 RAMEN ECHIKA FIT

8-4-13 Ginza, Chuo-ku
3981 3808
echika-echikafit.com/tokyo/
Open Mon–Sun 11am–10.30pm
Ginza station, exit C4
[MAP p. 204 B3]

The long queue permanently snaking out of this ramen eatery is your first clue that your tastebuds are in for a treat. The minimal interior belies its staus as a Michelin star-rated establishment, but the to-die-for chicken ramen easily scored the top accolade. Bench top seats allow you to watch the chefs in action. The tori paitan is a silky, creamy, substantial chicken broth with tender sliced chicken and chewy firm soba noodles (unusual for a ramen) and it's worth any wait – you could be queuing for more than an hour at busy times. If you're extra hungry they also do a cheese risotto and a tsukumen (dipping noodles). Add kick to your ramen with the miso extra called 'pungency widening' and order a soy egg to go perfectly with the sweet broth. Tie on a paper bib and tuck in. It's cash only. If the queue is too much, lucky you as next door is equally rated ramen joint Ginza Kazami. Opens June 2019.

IN & AROUND TOKYO STATION

Anchored by the Imperial Palace – one of Tokyo's most enduring icons – and its delightful gardens, Marunouchi is part business district, part cultural mecca, with some of Tokyo's poshest shops and most prestigious art galleries.

Nearby Tokyo Station is a sprawling gateway for the bullet trains that shoot off to every corner of Japan, the airport express and an alarming list of other train lines, but that doesn't mean it can't be fun. It's a frenetic underground world crammed with shops and restaurants. From here it's just a quick walk to Yurakucho (which is both the name of a precinct and a stretch of eateries) and the shopping delights that await within the massive flagship Muji department store.

→ Yurakucho Yokocho

1 IMPERIAL PALACE GARDEN/

1-1 Chiyoda, Tokyo
3213 1111
Open Tues–Thurs, Sat–Sun
9am–5pm
Otemachi station, exit C13a
or Tokyo station, exit for
Marunouchi North
[MAP p. 191 E2]

Once the site of Edo Castle, the Imperial Palace gardens are one of Tokyo's most beautiful green spaces and perfect for a walk, flower gazing (blooms make it spectacular in any season) or a picnic (grab supplies from **Tokyo Station** or **Rose Bakery**). Sights include the old castle guardhouse, moat, hefty Shimizu-mon gate, the Seimon Ishibashi 'Eyeglass' Bridge and three modern constructions: the **National Museum of Modern Art**, the **Science Museum** and popular concert space **The Nippon Budokan**. Other beautiful buildings include fairytale-like **Suwan Ochaya Teahouse** (sadly not open to the public) and the Imperial Palace itself, hidden amongst greenery which affords only glimpses. Northern garden **Chidorigafuchi** is a prime spot for cherry blossom viewing in April when crowds flock to enjoy the festive atmosphere. The gardens can be approached from any angle – factor in a day's visit to savour it all.

2 OEDO ANTIQUE MARKET

3-5-1 Marunouchi, Chiyoda
6407 6011
antique-market.jp
Open 1st and 3rd Sun
9am–4pm
Yurakucho station, exit for
International Forum
[MAP p. 204 B2]

Japanese antique collectors, flea market junkies, bin-riflers and crowd watchers have a perfect opportunity to get amongst it in Tokyo's biggest and busiest antique market. On the first and third Sundays of the month you can find 100–200 bustling stalls on the grounds of the Tokyo International Forum, south of Tokyo Station. The market has an extensive range of vintage Japanalia. If you're on the hunt for kimono, Kokeshi (homemade wooden folk-art dolls), hair pins, '60's and '70's toys, fans, pottery, furniture and various memorabilia, you'll definitely find it here. Remember, it's cash only, it's unlikely that they will organise shipping, bartering might be considered bad manners, and it will almost always be closed at the slightest hint of rain.

71

3 POSTALCO

2-2-1 Kyobashi Chuo
6262 6338
postalco.net
Open Mon–Sun 11am–8pm
Kyobashi station, exit 8
[MAP p. 204 C2]

A Tokyo–Brooklyn co-lab, Mike and Yu's philosophy to bring quality and beauty to utilitarian items is perfectly realised in Postalco's new Kyobashi store. An understated interior of clever lighting, warm wood, and vintage curiosities houses their collection of stylish, minimal, retro (with a modern twist) stationery, office organisers and lifestyle products. You'll find everything from a chic case for your glasses or fountain pen, notebooks, wallets, all your letter writing stationery, and that perfectly unusual key holder present for the favourite graphic designer in your life. You can even have your notebooks and other products customised. Postalco's take on rainwear has been ramped up a notch so your wet wardrobe is sorted. Collaborations with sought-after labels like Art and Science, Opening Ceremony and Issey Miyake give you an idea of how coveted their items are amongst Tokyo's design darlings. As an added bonus, if you love their aesthetic, book a night at **Hotel Claska**'s (see p. 165) new Postalco-designed room called 'Story'.

4 MUJI

3-8-3 Marunouchi, Chiyoda-ku
5208 8241
muji.com
Open Mon–Sun 10am–9pm
Yurakucho station, Kyobashi exit
[MAP p. 204 B2]

This Japanese retail giant is all about quality no-brand goods. It's everything you could want for your life, with no-fuss packaging, prices for the people and a design aesthetic that puts most other brands to shame. Sure, it's a global brand, but we're talking about the mother lode at this flagship store. Check out the 7000-plus products for sale in the lofty warehouse space set over three floors. You could come away with household goods, clothing, food, stationery and glasses to Muji up your life. Head up to the second floor for the **Muji cafe** and **Muji Atelier**, a gallery showcasing Muji's creative inspirations. And if you need some extra yen (you will), there's an international ATM on the ground floor.

73

5 TOKYO STATION

[MAP p. 204 B1]

Train stations are meant to be a way to get from A to B, but at Tokyo Station you might find yourself happily lost. Most of the action is at **First Avenue** at the Yaesu Underground Central exit. **Kitchen Street** is a labyrinth of small restaurants where some of Tokyo's culinary masters have stalls. Nearby **Okashi Land** has excellent sweet shops where you can buy beautifully packaged gifts. There are plenty of places selling bento boxes, perfect for taking on journeys. On **Ramen Street** you'll find eight popular noodle soup joints. If you don't eat meat, head east to **Keiyo Street** for **T's Tan Tan**, who do a vegan version of ramen. One floor down, the fun really kicks in. **Character Street** is an avenue of colourful stores, each devoted to the most beloved cartoon and anime characters. Take your kids here and they'll love you forever. Ultraman, Hello Kitty, Miffy and Moomin will all compete for your kids' attention in bold, bright and very loud stores. This majestic station even has a hotel and gallery. 'Tip of the iceberg' comes to mind. If you get totally lost, head straight to the station concierge!

POCKET TIP

Grab a bento box from Tokyo Station and head to the Imperial Palace gardens for a picnic.

6 IPPODO

1F, Kokusai building 3-1-1
Marunouchi, Chiyoda
6212 0202
ippodo-tea.co.jp
Open Mon–Sun 11am–7pm
Tokyo station, Marunouchi
south exit
[MAP p. 204 A2]

Three centuries of selling tea, 'blessed by mother nature' and picked in fertile tea fields has made Ippodo the most famous tea house in Kyoto. You can get the quintessential Kyoto tea experience at this beautiful Tokyo store and attached teahouse **Kaboku**. Join the counter queue and ask the knowledgeable staff about their extensive range of packaged teas: Sencha, Matcha, Hojicha, Genmaicha and more. If you are curious about which teas are cultivated in the shade or in the open-field, ask for a tea tasting. Or join the cafe queue for a leisurely experience. Staff will help you find the right tea for your tastes. They'll throw terms around like 'tea leaves unravelling', 'do not agitate' and 'the last drop is best'. Your tea will come with seasonal wagashi (Japanese sweets) or you can prepare it yourself (under strict instructions and a timer). Ippodo also sell teapots, whisks, cups and canisters – for fine gifts. Order a take-out Matcha latte in winter or a cold green tea latte in summer.

75

7 SAKE SHOP FUKUMITSUYA MARUNOUCHI

1F, Kokusai building 3-1-1
Marunouchi, Chiyoda
5288 5015
fukumitsuya.co.jp
Open Mon–Sun 10am–7pm
Tokyo station, Marunouchi
south exit
[MAP p. 204 A2]

Discovering the true joy of sake is one of Tokyo's must-do experiences and Fukumitsuya is one of the premium places to immerse yourself in sake culture. It specialises in 'Junmai' sake from the Eastern coastal prefecture of Kanazawa. Junmai is a pure form of sake mainly made with rice and water, so Kanazawa's crisp water source allows for the perfect alchemy. Keep a look out for the cute sake barrel logo and head inside. You can try before you buy, find what appeals to your palate and buy a bottle or two. There is also a range of other products from cups and vessels to a sake-based beauty range. Try the take-out sake ice-cream and a warm amazake (a very low alcohol form of sake) and yuzu drink, perfect on a cold day. If you're undecided, pop into the bar across the corridor for the tasting set of three different sake varieties. Staff will happily fill you in on the processes involved in producing the excellent tipple.

8 NIHONBA∫HI YUKARI

3-2-14 Nihonbashi, Chuo-ku
3271 3436
nihonbashi-yukari.com
Open Mon–Sat 11am–2pm &
5–10pm
Tokyo station, Yaesu exit
[MAP p. 204 C1]

Nihonbashi Yukari is owned and run by Kimio Nonaga, former champion of the Japanese television cooking show *Iron Chef*. If you think this means you're in for an expensive meal, think again. For around ¥4000 you can get the seasonal deluxe bento lunch (order in advance when you make your reservation). Ours included melt-in-the-mouth sashimi and tofu, tasting plates of grilled meats and other elegant dishes artfully arranged with delicate flower garnishes. Each small exquisite course of the bento banquet will make you feel like you're dining with the emperor, or at least Chairman Kaga (aka Shigekatsu Katsuta, host of *Iron Chef*). This is an experience you'll never forget for a price you'll barely notice.

9 YURAKUCHO & YURAKU CONCOURſE

4-3-3 Sotokanda, Chiyoda-ku
5298 5411
Open Mon–Sun 10am–5pm
Yurakucho station,
Central west exit
[MAP p. 204 A2]

Under Yurakucho station and the rumble of passing trains you'll find Yurakucho, a 700-metre-long row of charming old-school bars and eateries. It looks really amazing at night, as street lamps light up and roller doors reveal previously hidden yakitori (grilled skewered meats) and ramen (noodle soup) joints, made for in-and-out drinking and dining, where workers can grab a quick bite before heading home.

At the end of the Yurakucho line of bars and eateries is the Yuraku Concourse tunnel, which has some good standing bars. Pop in for a few drinks (if you can still stand that is). Peeling and faded Japanese movie posters seem to hold Yuraku Concourse together and old signs and low-lit paper lanterns recall the Tokyo of days gone by.

AKIHABARA

Firmly rooted in the 21st century, Akiba, as the locals call it, is a mecca for tech junkies and obsessive fans of anime and manga. It's not nicknamed 'Electric Town' for nothing: you can glimpse the future in electronics here and score the latest newfangled gadgets. If figurines, computers and vintage toys are your bag, you've hit the jackpot.

The pulsating thoroughfare of Chuo Dori is a riot of flashing lights, electronic noise, cartoon-colour buildings, toy vending machines and all-night wi-fi booths. The coffee shops here sell bottomless cups to keep you wired all day, and pastries in the shapes of anime characters are sold everywhere. Chances are, if you put on your Astro Boy outfit and go for a stroll, no-one will bat an eyelid.

→ *The Canned Oden corner in Akihabara*

1 NATSUGE MUSEUM

2-13-3 Kanda, Sakumacho
t-tax.net
Opening hours vary, check
website
Akihabara station, Showa
Dori exit
[MAP p. 205 B4]

Serious retro gamers make a bee-line (or a Pac-Man chomp) to Natsuge, an 'interactive' museum where you can actually play on classic consoles, video games and computers from days gone by. Restored to perfect working order, these retro game machines date back as far as – gulp – the eighties! That's thirty plus years, long enough to provoke some serious feelings of nostalgia, hence the name – Natsuge, a compound for 'natsukashi', which is Japanese for 'nostalgia' or 'fond rememberance', 'museum' and 'game'. Here you get a room crammed with Frogger, Space Invaders, Galaga, Gauntlet and Submarine – less of a museum, more of a classic game arcade. Speakers pump out the sounds and the music while a wall of signatures from famous game makers, writers and animators provides the historical footnotes.

POCKET TIP
Visit Radio Kaikan, a ten-storey Akihabara institution selling everything electronics and manga.

2 YELLOW SUBMARINE

6F, Radio Kaikan building,
1-15-16 Sotokanda, Chiyoda-ku
3526 3828
Open Mon–Sun 11.30am–9pm
Akihabara station, Electric Town
exit
[MAP p. 205 B4]

This is not a store for collectors of The Beatles memorabilia as the iconic logo might suggest, but a model builder's utopia. The shop is wall-to-wall glass cases and shelves crammed with assorted kits to build tanks, ships, aeroplanes, dinosaurs, spaceships and creatures from sci-fi films. The range starts from easy-to-assemble and works its way up to way-too-many-pieces. A mostly male clientele of deadly serious modellers wanders the store with furrowed brows sizing up their next purchase. Much of the store is a museum showing detailed, ready-assembled versions of what's for sale, assembled by known Japanese modellers. Whether you'll be able to put them together with the same skill is another thing, but it's all about the journey, right?

3 *S*UPER POTATO

3F, Kitabayashi Building,
1-11-2 Sotokanda, Chiyoda-ku
5298 5411
Open Mon–Fri 11am–8pm,
Sat–Sun 10am–8pm
Akihabara station, Electric Town
exit
[MAP p. 205 A3]

Analog fans rejoice! Donkey Kong and Pac-Man are alive and well in this alternate retail universe. Super Potato is the *Back to the Future* of shopping, with three colourful floors of obsolete video games, consoles and figurines. Prices might be on the steep side, but where else are you going to get your hands on outmoded Nintendo 64, Xbox and PlayStation games all restored to perfect working order? Super Potato's top floor has vintage arcade games – you can eat like an eighties gamer! They sell '80s Japanese snacks and sweets and hot water for Ramen noodle pots. Just when you thought the games of the not-too-distant past were gone forever, they live to be played another day! The bleeps and bloops stay with you even after you leave the store, and you'll be humming the Super Mario theme all the way home.

4 MANDARAKE

3-11-12 Sotokanda, Chiyoda-ku
3252 7007
mandarake.co.jp
Open Mon–Sun 12pm–8pm
Akihabara station, Electric Town exit
[MAP p. 205 A3]

Mandarake's flagship store pretty much sums up Akihabara. This uber-geek wonderland is a maze of narrow stairwells, cluttered shelves and teetering boxes, almost mimicking an Escher painting. If you're on the hunt for anime, manga, toys, creepy-cute dolls, graphic novels or figurines, then your spaceship has landed. Vintage is big here, so if you like your collectibles with a retro feel, you're sure to find that action figure or sci-fi swap card on your wish list. Warning! Warning! If you're here with junior, avoid the very graphic anime on the fourth floor, unless you want to start the birds and the bees talk early.

85

5 DON QUIJOTE

4-3-3 Sotokanda, Chiyoda-ku
5298 5411
Open Mon–Sun 10am–5am
Akihabara station, Electric
Town exit
[MAP p. 205 A3]

Donki, as it is affectionately known, is an out-of-control discount superstore. Look for the blue penguin mascot on Chuo Dori; he'll point the way to this retail maze of precariously balanced piles of toys, comics, homewares, alcohol and dubious pharmaceuticals. Impulse buyers won't know which way to turn. It's probably more trash than treasure, but food, gag gifts, electrical appliances, souvenirs and even luxury brand items all get the bargain treatment, and rifling through the seemingly endless stock is great fun. Be careful where you walk: turn one corner near fluffy animals and you could find yourself in an aisle full of sex toys! Note: the store is open until 5am for those times you urgently require a pair of clip-on cat ears.

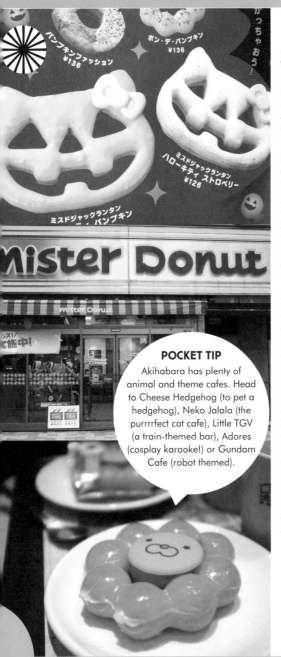

6 MISTER DONUT

3-13 Sotokanda, Chiyoda-ku
3255 1655
Open Mon–Sun 8.30am–7pm
Akihabara station, Electric Town exit
[MAP p. 205 A3]

If your secret shame is a *Twin Peaks* diner-style dripolator coffee in a bottomless cup partnered with some sweet fried dough, then this is the place for you. Mister Donut has a charming old-school feel with its vintage Americana signage and interior. This being Japan though, they love to 'character up' their doughnuts. If you're lucky enough to visit during a special holiday like Halloween, your doughnut could be a ghost or a vampire. The pick of the bunch is the 'Pon de Lion', with its adorable lion face and dough-ball mane. The green-tea-and-bitter-chocolate-filled versions are also popular buys, as are the honey churros. If you're a coffee snob or doughnut connoisseur, perhaps give this place a miss. But if you like your snacks cheap and colourful, get yourself a Misdoclub card and start earning yourself some free dough!

POCKET TIP

Akihabara has plenty of animal and theme cafes. Head to Cheese Hedgehog (to pet a hedgehog), Neko Jalala (the purrrrfect cat cafe), Little TGV (a train-themed bar), Adores (cosplay karaoke!) or Gundam Cafe (robot themed).

7 GAME BAR A BUTTON

1-13-9 Taito, Taito-ku
5856 5475
Open Mon–Fri 5pm–12am,
Sat–Sun 5pm–4am
Akihabara station,
Showa Dori exit
[MAP p. 205 C3]

You'll have to make like Pac-Man and chomp your way through Akihabara's streets to uncover this playful bar. A tiny brick building wedged between houses and high-rise apartments, Game Bar a Button has everything you need if you are into the combined pursuits of retro gaming and drinking. Vintage games, consoles and all manner of related equipment line the walls and benches of this bar. A mix of game fans and industry types swap stories about the good old days of video gaming as they down cold beers. A giant screen is hooked up to some retro consoles and you can plug in and play some genuine classics. It's the perfect place to toast the history of computer gaming!

8 RAMEN TENJINSHITA DAIKI

2-4-4 Taito, Taito-ku,
3834 0348
daiki1999.com
Open Mon–Fri 11am–2.30pm
& 6–10pm; Sat 11am–3pm &
5.30–8.30pm
Akihabara station, Showa
Dori exit
[MAP p. 205 C3]

Tenjinshita's tasty ramen (noodle soup) is a contrast to the many fast food and junk food joints of Akihabara, which has long had a reputation for 'B-Style' foods – everything to fuel the Otaku (obsessive fan and collector) on the go, something to grab quickly while mid-collectible, electronic gadget or manga hunting. Ramen is quick, cheap and tasty, but it's far from B-style. Tenjinshita Daiki specialises in Shoyu ramen, a soy-sauce-based irresistible bowl of noodles immersed in soup topped with chashu pork. Other favourites include two chicken-based ramens, one light, one heavy, according to your preference and a tsukumen where noodles are separate from the broth and added according to your taste. Join the perpetual line and find your favourite and see why ramen is starting to make some serious noise in Akihabara (mainly slurping).

POCKET TIP
Walk the side streets to Ramen Tenjinshita Daiki to find so many great eateries.

そば(細麺)
Tori-soba
¥950

純とりそば(細麺)
Jun Tori-soba
¥950

特製純とりそば(細麺)
Tokusei Jun Tori-soba
¥1100

うめしおらーめん(細麺)
Ume-sio Ramen
¥900

特製うめしおらーめん
Tokusei Ume-sio
¥

ーめん
¥980

納豆らーめん
Natto ramen
¥900

特製納豆らーめん
Tokusei Natto ramen
¥1100

¥900

めん
¥1050

大盛つけめん
Oomori Tukemen
¥950

特製大盛つけめん
Tokusei Oomori Tukemen
¥1150

トッピング
ちゃーしゅう
¥300

トッピング
味付たま
¥300

担々麺
v. 玉入
¥1050

トッピング
ちゃーしゅう
¥300

トッピング
味付たま
¥

冷やしとりそば
¥950

ごはん

自家製ぬか漬

とりめし

UENO, ASAKUSA & YANAKA

If you're after a taste of traditional Japan, head to Asakusa, whose temples and shrines give an impressive glimpse into the beauty of old Japan. It's also a tourist mecca where traditional Japanese culture meets contemporary madness.

Grab a grilled octopus tentacle on a stick and fire up your camera – photo opportunities are everywhere here, from the majestic temple Senso-ji to the towering new kid on the block, the Tokyo Skytree building. The streets and walkways are dotted with long-standing eateries, specialist snack stands and established souvenir shops. Surrounding areas Ueno and Yanaka are rich with history and have some of the finest museums, parks and traditional paper stores in the city.

→ï One of Asakusa's old-school eateries

1 UENO & ASAKUSA SIGHTS

[MAP p. 206 and 207]

Asakusa's **Senso-ji**, a Buddhist temple built in 645, has a five-tiered pagoda, two striking gates, voluminous lanterns and a festive, street-stall-strewn walkway. Nearby **Tokyo Skytree** is a transcendent spire offering views of Tokyo's expanse. **Ueno Park** has some of Tokyo's best museums and galleries. **Shinobazu Pond** comes alive during sakura (cherry blossom) season when couples in swan boats float among lotus flowers under pink blossoms. The **Tokyo National Museum** has the largest collection of traditional Japanese art in the city. The **National Museum of Western Art**, designed by Le Corbusier, is a modernist masterpiece. The **National Museum of Nature and Science** has a taxidermy of Hachicko the loyal dog (*see* p. 2). The park has so much – the **Shitamachi Museum** (exploring life in Tokyo's poorer downtown district in the early 1800's), the **Tokyo Metropolitan Art Museum**, **Ueno Zoo** (pandas and a spectacular pagoda) and shrines: **Kaneiji**, **Kiyomizu Kannon**, **Bentendo** and **Toshogu**.

POCKET TIP

If you're at Asakusa station, don't miss Tokyo Skytree and the Asahi Beer Hall skyline – one of the world's great pop-photo opportunities.

2 YANAKA CEMETERY

7-5-24 Yanaka
Taito, Tokyo
Open Mon–Sun,
8.30am–5.15pm
Nippori station
[MAP p. 206 C1]

Walking through Yanaka Cemetery (Yanaka Spirit Park) is a magical experience, at dusk the Yanaka cats slink among the gravestones and the setting sun gives it a haunting stillness. Its infamous history includes a five-tiered pagoda, burnt down in an arson/double suicide case in 1957 featured in Kodarahan's novel *The Five-Storied Pagoda*. At the entrance is the enchanting Meiji era flower shop, **Hanaju**, which dates back to 1870 and sells flowers and small brooms for sweeping graves clean. The autumn colours and cherry blossoms in season make the cemetery resplendent – if you're here during sakura snow, the pink blossoms drift down and blanket the graves. Famous people are interred here, including last shogun Tokugawa Yoshinobu and novelist Ichiyo Higuchi who appears on the ¥5,000 note. It is even more haunting (and moving) during Obon, the festival of the dead on July 15th, when families call out to the souls of the dead.

3 ISETATSU

2-18-9 Yanaka, Taito-ku
3823 1453
Open Mon–Sun 11am–7pm
Sendagi station, exit 1
[MAP p. 206 A1]

Isetatsu was established in 1864 and it's still owned and run by the founding family, now in its fifth generation. It's actually two beautiful stores just a few doors away from each other, which use traditional methods to make chiyogami (wood-block-printed paper). Paper lovers will be in heaven with the stores' endless array of beautifully printed and patterned paper, kept in large wooden drawers and bought in large sheets. Themes usually relate to nature: brightly coloured flowers, leaves, seasons and fanciful tableaux of animals doing people-type things. Chiyogami used to be made into toys for children, but now it's best framed and transformed into high art. If you are looking for souvenirs, the two stores also have a range of delightful stationery, paper fans, mobiles, greeting cards and good-luck charms.

4 KAPPABA/HI DORI

Between Asakusa and Ueno stations, Tawaramachi station, exit 3
[MAP p. 207 A3]

The thoroughfare of Kappabashi Dori will literally 'cater' to your every need. Look up to see the giant chef's head with the perfectly coiffured moustache and you'll know you're entering the biggest cookware street-slash-market in the world. Tokyo has around 80,000 restaurants, and this is where their chefs shop. Leaving no stone unturned, each store has a mind-boggling array of ceramics, cutlery, crockery, utensils, chopsticks, chef uniforms, tableware and just about anything else you can think of that relates to the art, or the business, of cookery.

Make sure you check out the famous sampuru (from the English word 'sample') – the plastic display food that adorns the windows of many Japanese restaurants. Like '70s frozen moments, sampuru range from the functional to the fabulous, the comical to the disturbing – they're like little bits of pop art and make for interesting souvenirs. Now's the time to start your obsession for Japanese home cooking. At the very least you'll find some pretty things to beautify your home.

95

5 AMEYA-YOKOCHO

Between Ueno and
Okachimachi stations
Ueno station, south exit
[MAP p. 205 B1]

Springing up in the black
market years following World
War Two, this narrow winding
alley below the elevated
train track between Ueno
and Okachimachi stations is
noisy, crowded and wears its
old seedy charm with pride.
Ameya-Yokocho is still an
open-air market for locals,
so make the most of it and
grab something fresh to take
into Ueno Park for lunch.
Alternatively, slide yourself into
one of the many inexpensive
and delicious tempura, yakitori
(grilled skewered chicken) or
ramen (noodle soup) joints,
and sample some seafood,
which the market is known
for. Food carts, stand-up bars
and eateries are crammed into
every available niche, ensuring
no real estate goes to waste.
Park yourself on a bench and
order beer and whatever's
going; it's all good, clean,
slightly seedy fun.

POCKET TIP
The Skyliner train goes
from Ueno to the Narita
airport, so if you need to
while away some hours
before a flight, put your bag
in a locker at the Keisei-
Ueno station (across from
the main Ueno station).

6 CIBI CAFE & DESIGN STORE

3-37-11 Sendagi, Bunkyo
5834 8045
cibi.jp
Open Mon–Sun 8am–6pm
Nippori station
[MAP p. 206 A1]

Already a favourite in our hometown of Melbourne, Cibi cafe, run by Zenta and Meg Tanaka, is a home-away-from-home, where simple and delicious home-cooked meals put a smile on your face and a perfectly curated selection of homewares put style into your home. The Tokyo branch of Cibi cements their reputation for bringing family love to the street cafe and where better for it to be located than in the backstreets of Yanaka – fast becoming Tokyo's coolest off-the-grid destination. Western flavours add allure to traditional family recipes. Deceptively simple, Cibi is all about head, hands and heart and satisfies all three. Pull up a chair and feast on their Japanese breakfasts, delicious lunch plates, sandwiches, muffins and cakes while watching local Tokyo filter through the charming narrow Yanaka backstreets.

POCKET TIP

Scai the Bathhouse is an amazing old Sento (bath house) that has been converted into one of Tokyo's coolest new contemporary gallery spaces.

7 ASAKUSA EATING

Asakusa station, exit A4
[MAP p. 207 B3]

Much of old Asakusa remains unchanged and you can eat at long-standing noodle houses, tempura joints and yakitori (grilled skewered chicken) specialists. Check out **Namiki Yabu Soba** for authentic 'worker' soba noodles (closed on Thursdays.) For ramen (noodle soups), try the fresh handmade ones at **Bazoku**. For the fried tasty goodness of tempura, join the locals at **Sansada**, which has been around for 150 years! Fans of deep-fried pork should hit **Katsukichi**, which has 50 different types of tonkatsu. Eel enthusiasts can get top-notch unagi at **Hatsuogawa**. Tokyo's oldest onigiri place, **Yadoroku** has perfected these popular rice triangles over its 60 years. For a sweet-tooth, head to **Nishiyama**, serving wagashi (traditional Japanese sweets) since the 1850s. **Nakamise dori** which leads up to Senso-ji has an amazing array of snacks (sweet potato soft cream, wagashi sweets and rice crackers). Long-standing, family-owned wagashi shops are a spiritual crusade in Asakusa. Try **Usagiya** for the perfect doryaki (red bean) establishment, perfecting their craft since 1914, or queue up at **Kamejyu**.

POCKET TIP
If you're not sure about where to go, just join a queue.

8 HAGISO

3-10-25 Yanaka, Taito-ku
5832 9808
Open Mon–Sun 11am–11pm
Sendagi station, exit 1
[MAP p. 206 A1]

While Hagiso still has some rustic charm from centuries ago – wooden beams and pillars of the old house remain – this is essentially new Yanaka. The cafe has been updated with clean, minimalist lines and the food is rustic-modern with only a slight nod towards traditional Japanese fare. It's a great place to while away an afternoon on your laptop with young locals. A contemporary gallery sits astride the cafe, so you can check out some challenging contemporary art while downing some booze or munching on cake and coffee. Lunch sets are good value, and the keema curry, delicious with a fried egg plonked on top, goes down well with one of Hagiso's craft beers at night.

POCKET TIP

Mimi NoYu Cafe has its own foot bath – so soak tired tootsies before having a restorative cup of tea.

SHINJUKU

Shinjuku is a chaotic precinct of stark contrasts. Its station has 200 exits and around 3.5 million people go through it every day, which should give you some idea of what you are in for! Sure, Shinjuku is a bit rough around the edges, but its manic nature makes it one of Tokyo's most popular destinations. Every brand, label and chain store has an outlet here, creating a seemingly endless crowd of shoppers.

It's not all madness though: some truly beautiful relics of old Tokyo butt up against the colossal superstructures. Take some time out and stroll through the peaceful gardens of Shinjuku Gyoen or head up the Metropolitan Government Building for a view that stretches to Mount Fuji.

→ *Shinjuku station*

SIGHTS
1. Shinjuku Gyoen
2. Golden Gai

SHOPPING
3. Disc Union
4. Bingoya
5. Isetan

SHOPPING & EATING
6. NEWoMan

EATING & DRINKING
7. Calico Cat
8. Tempura Tsunahachi
9. Samurai

1 SHINJUKU GYOEN

11 Naitomachi, Shinjuku
3350 0151
env.go.jp/garden/shinjukugyoen
Open Tues–Sun 9am–4pm
Shinjuku station, south exit
[MAP p. 202 C4]

Escape the maze of tunnels of Shinjuku station and take sanctuary at Shinjuku Gyoen. Once the private playground for feudal lords and emperors, dating back to the 1600s, the park was rebuilt and replanted after World War Two as a park of the people. It has 20,000 trees, expansive lawns, ponds, wilderness walks, tea houses, restaurants and a greenhouse, plus English-, French- and Japanese-themed gardens. Grab a bento from **Kakiyasu Gyumeshi** and have a picnic. The traditional tea-houses, **Rakuutei** or **Shoutentei**, provide exquisite tea and wagashi (traditional Japanese sweets). Wildly popular during sakura (cherry blossom) season, people flock to picnic under around 1,000 trees. The park also boasts a famous chrysanthemum show (early November), and is stunning when the leaves of the sycamore, maple, cherry, dogwood and ginko turn the park several shades of red for autumn.

POCKET TIP

With all that Shinjuku station foot traffic, the precinct is naturally a ramen hotspot. Head to Men'ya Musashi, Tatsunoya, Yakia Goshio, Nagi, Ramen Jiro, Man'ya Sho or Tsukumen Gonokami Seisakusho, for a bowl of the best.

POCKET TIP
The Metropolitan Government Building has a stunning (and free) panoramic view over Tokyo from the 45th floor.

2 GOLDEN GAI

Shinjuku station, east exit
[MAP p. 202 B2]

This popular night-life district is a charming and disorderly remnant of pre-World War Two Tokyo, towered over by the high-rise behemoths of modern Shinjuku. Entering Golden Gai is like being a mouse in a maze and that's not just because of the area's network of tiny alleys and lanes. It's also due to the experiments you'll be participating in as you enter each weird and wonderful drinking establishment. There are over 200 bars crammed into this unique drinking zone, so we can only give you a teensy taster of what's on offer.

For starters, there's the very cool **Albatross G**, where chandeliers, crucifixes and stuffed animal heads vibrate to some choice indie rock tunes. Also check out oddball **Bar Plastic Model** and drink enough to actually solve a Rubik's Cube. Then there's the downright disturbing **Tachibana Shinsatsushitsu**, where you can order medical-themed cocktails (colonic irrigation anyone?) and admire the giant silicon penis on the counter.

103

3 DISC UNION

4F/5F, Shimogiku building,
3-34-12, Shinjukuku
3352 2141
Open Mon–Sun 11am–9pm
Shinjuku station, east Central
exit
[MAP p. 202 B3]

For the music enthusiast, a day will not be enough in this super-sized labyrinth of CDs, DVDs and vinyl. If you can't find what you want here, you must have the most obscure taste in the world. There are 7 floors in total, but the top floor is a collector's dream. Watch as people flick through racks of records before getting misty-eyed and gleefully grabbing that long-sought-after pop or rock Holy Grail. Genres jump from indie, jazz, hip-hop and punk to heavy metal, soul and disco. The test pressings lining the walls will make your jaw drop, both for their rarity and price. This is the flagship store, but Disc Union specialist music stores are dotted elsewhere around Tokyo. All worth a visit, they're tiny oddball enclaves where you'll lose hours searching for that special dub, house or death-metal find.

POCKET TIP
Sunday Bake Shop is a must-visit for lovers of baked goods.

4 BINGOYA

10-6 Wakamatsu-cho, Shinjuku
3202 8778
bingoya.tokyo
Open Tues–Sun 10am–7pm
Opening hours can vary,
check website
[MAP p. 203 B2]

Bingoya is the perfect one-stop shop for Japanese crafts of all kinds, spread over 5 floors. If you're on the hunt for noren curtains, kimono, furoshiki (Japanese wrapping cloth), pottery and ceramics, stationery, lamps, fans, textiles and furniture, you'll find it all here. The basement specialises in folk children's toys, Kokeshi dolls and clay- and iron-ware and the fourth floor features more upmarket buys in the lacquerware and traditional Japanese cook and kitchenware categories. Rooms are small and charming and the levels reveal various items as you climb. Grab a basket and start stocking up, there's souvenirs and keepsakes aplenty in this perfectly selected and curated haul.

5 ISETAN

3-14-1, Shinjuku, Shinjukuku
3352 1111
isetan.mistore.jp/shinjuku
Open Mon–Sun 10.30am–8pm
Shinjuku station, east exit
[MAP p. 202 B2]

Isetan department store is friendly, relaxed and quite 'with it', considering it's over 100 years old. Spread over eight buildings, you'll find designer fashions with eye-popping displays, kimonos and obis (sashes) in sumptuous fabrics and a generally more luxe take on the usual department-store fare. The real attraction here is the stunning food hall, a posh basement venue that is a mouth-watering journey through Japanese and international cuisine. It definitely leans more towards all things French, but the perfect rows of Japanese sweets are so alluring you might think you've stumbled into the jewellery department.

6 NEWOMAN

4-1-6 Shinjuku, Shinjuku,
3352 1120
newoman.jp
Open Mon–Sun 11am–8pm
[MAP p. 202 A3]

On the east side of the station
is a snapshot of the chic,
grown-up side of Shinjuku.
It features boutique fashion
stores, cafes and the best
in Tokyo food, homewares,
fashion and lifestyle. Tokyo
premium food stores like rice
specialist **Akomeya**, wagashi
(traditional Japanese sweets)
purveyor **Toraya** (they have a
branch of **Toraya An Stand**
here, *see* p. 33) and **Bluebottle
Coffee** will fuel your shopping
spree. There's updated
versions of fashion favourites
like **Beams News, Prefer
Ships** and **Salon Adam
Et Rope**. Cosmetic and skin
care specialists **Shiro +** have
beautiful products that use
unusual Japanese ingredients
like rice and yuzu. Head to
Fruit Couture Takano in the
food hall for irresistible (and
well-dressed) fruit desserts,
Wa Sandwich for a Tokyo
take on the lunch staple
or **Komeyano OnigiriYa
Kikutaya Beikokuten** for
an elevated version of the
rice triangle.

7 CALICO CAT

5F, 1-16-2 Kabukicho,
Shinjuku-ku
6457 6387
catcafe.jp/shop_shinuku
Open Mon–Sun 10am–5pm
Shinjuku station, west exit
[MAP p. 202 A2]

If you want some Tokyo cute
overload, make sure you drop
into Calico Cat. One of those
only-in-Tokyo experiences, this
cafe caters for the cat deprived.
It's hard to spot the building,
so look up to find the colourful
sign, then shimmy into the
two-person lift and head up to
the fifth floor. Cats of all shapes,
sizes, colours and breeds go
about their daily business here,
occasionally attended by the
staff (the expression 'dogs have
owners, cats have staff' has
never been so appropriate).
You can stroke the animals
and take pictures, but there's
no picking up! Enjoy coffee
and cake as you admire the
furry felines, but be prepared
for them to spend a lot of time
sleeping … as cats do.

POCKET TIP
Haruki Murakami fans,
head to Shinjuku's
Nakamuraya Café,
featured in *IQ84*
and DUG featured in
Norwegian Wood.

8 TEMPURA TSUNAHACHI

3-31-8 Shinjuku, Shinjukuku
3352 1012
tunahachi.co.jp
Open Mon–Sun 11am–10.30pm
Shinjuku station, west exit
[MAP p. 202 A2]

This old-world tempura restaurant must have seen some changes since it was set up in a meandering two-storey Japanese house in 1950, but it ignores the encroaching skyscrapers and retail giants and goes about its business of providing excellent tempura to a hungry crowd. Service here is fast and friendly. Delicate crispy tempura pieces arrive with a trio of salts; the wasabi and black kombu (seaweed) salts are especially delicious. We recommend grabbing a seat at the bar and ordering the tempura à la carte to watch the chef in action; the prawn, pumpkin and aubergine tempura are all awesome. The set lunch is a seriously good deal for the crispy light tempura and a memorable delicate miso with tiny clams.

9 ſAMURAI

5F, 3-35-5 Shinjuku, Shinjukuku
3341 0383
Open Mon–Sun 6pm–1am
Shinjuku station, south exit
[MAP p. 202 B3]

You know you're in Tokyo when you get out of an elevator on the fifth floor of a nondescript building to find one of the hippest bars in the world. The first thing you'll undoubtedly notice are the thousand or so lucky cat statues. Beyond that is a room full of jazz regalia, with posters and photos lining the walls and shelves stuffed with records. Unusually for Tokyo it's quite a big space, so the whole gang can easily come along. The drinks are well priced and the vibe, helped along by a jazz soundtrack, is relaxed rather than pretentious. Be mindful of the table charge – around ¥300 from 6pm to 9pm and ¥500 after nine – but really, who cares? When the drinking is this cool, everything else just fades into insignificance.

KOENJI

Largely unaffected by World War Two bombing and the '80s construction frenzy, Koenji has the charming look and feel of pre-boom Japan. Its relaxed atmosphere hides a swirling youth undercurrent, and Koenji's late-night bars and 'live houses' (live-music venues) generate a vibrant music scene. There are also more than 70 vintage stores on Koenji's crisscross network of streets, making it a great place to spend the day trawling for retro gear.

Take a coffee break along the way: Koenji has some of Tokyo's most unique cafes. Ramen (noodle soup) and yakitori (grilled skewered meat) joints crowd the streets around the station, and you'll find some of Tokyo's most creative types playing up a storm in tiny, hidden bars late at night.

→ *Lover Soul vintage store on Look Street*

SIGHTS
1. Live Houses

SHOPPING
2. Be-in Record
3. Vintage Shopping in Koenji

EATING & DRINKING
4. Floresta Nature Doughnuts
5. Hattifnatt
6. Dizz
7. Coffee House Poem

1 LIVE HOUSES

[MAP p. 209]

Koenji is well known for its live houses, underground dive bars and music obsessed watering holes where bands sweat it out on small stages, giving their all for punters who enthusiastically swill booze and immerse themselves in the sounds. Punk, electronica, punk electronica, jazz fusion, electronic jazz fusion, progressive metal, jingly jangly cute pop, jingly jangly cute pop metal – it's all on display and changes dramatically from one day to the next in different venues. You won't know what you're getting, but you know it will be great, or in the very least an experience … Popular joints include **Koenji High**, **UFO Club**, **20,000 Den Atsu**, **Penguin House**, **Sound Studio Dom** and **Muryoko Muzenji**.

2 BE-IN RECORD

2F, 3-57-8 Koenji, Suginami-ku
3316 3700
bein.co.jp
Open Mon–Sun
12.30pm–8.30pm
Koenji station
[MAP p. 209 A2]

Be-In Record is a treasure trove of collectible vinyl, a haven for the obsessive fan of first releases and test pressings. Music aficionados will have a minor meltdown here as they madly rifle through the amazing collection (Beatles and Stones fans, in particular, will be in seventh heaven). When they finally raise their heads, hours will have past, food will be needed and bored partners will be long gone. Boxes crammed with records take up most of the room; there's barely space to squeeze between them, but true music lovers won't be bothered by that. Most genres are covered, including rock, pop, punk, R&B, soul, jazz and heavy metal, and extending to psych, garage and '60s freakbeat. There's plenty of indie as well. Prices for the premium products can definitely be on the steep side, but serious collectors won't mind paying. And for music buffs with limited funds, there are still some great affordable finds amongst the impressive range.

115

3 VINTAGE SHOPPING IN KOENJI

Koenji station, south exit
[MAP p. 209 A2]

Vintage hunters beware: you'll be hyperventilating on every street corner in this pre-loved paradise. If you want to dress like Jagger, swing in '60s London gear, groove like a San Francisco hippie or put your hands in the air at a '90s rave, someone in Koenji will have your subculture covered. At last count there were over 70 vintage stores in this small precinct, with a staggering diversity. And it's not just clothes either. If you are looking for that Raggedy Ann doll to add to your collection, a classic Pyrex mug or a Beatles test pressing, we'll be surprised if you don't come up trumps.

The best way to tackle shopping in Koenji is to set a few hours aside and just wander, popping into stores as you come across them. **Look Street** and **Central Road** are good places to start. Most importantly, remember to look up, as many stores are on the second and third floors. Side streets and alleyways are also worth peering down in search of an alluring sign.

4 FLORESTA NATURE DOUGHNUTƧ

3-34-14 Koenjikita, Suginami-ku
5356 5656
Open Mon–Sun 9am–8pm
Koenji station
[MAP p. 209 B1]

Described by Floresta as the 'guilt free' or 'nature' doughnut, these tasty treats are organic and handmade in-store. If you're in the market for a doughnut though, health benefits are probably not the first thing on your mind. The animal doughnuts are the major drawcard, and people flock here to try sweet dough in the shape of panda bears, smiling cats, rabbits, frogs and tigers, to name but a few. Little details like crunchy ears sweeten the deal further. These are pretty much the cutest looking doughnuts you'll ever see, treats to make your heart melt, but not your wallet. And, of course, they're delicious, especially with an afternoon coffee. On hot days try a granita, which comes with a tiny doughnut creature bobbing on top, so cute you won't want to eat it. No doubt your tastebuds will win out in the end, so make sure you snap some pictures first!

5 HATTIFNATT

2-18-10 Koenjikita, Suginami-ku
6762 8122
Open Mon–Sat 12pm–12am,
Sun 12pm–11pm
Koenji station
[MAP p. 209 B1]

Watch your head as you enter: the cafe door is like an entrance to a pixie house. Based on the creatures from the *Moomins*, this cafe is a children's storybook brought to life. The fairytale theme continues as you climb the narrow stairs and head into the 'tree house', a cute wooden room with stepladders that lead to tiny tatami spaces. The walls are covered with naive art, brightly coloured children's pictures that make the place look a bit like a nursery. This makes the hardcore alcohol on the menu a bit confusing, but it's the inner child they're going for here, so sit back and wrap your hands around a hot mug of 'glamour nanna' coffee and Baileys. You can also get food here, mostly pizza, pies and cake; press the buzzer to summon your waiter when you're ready to order. If you've been on the Baileys, be careful when you head back down the stairs: they're steep!

6 DIZZ

3-5-17 Koenjikita, Suginami-ku
3336 2545
Open Mon–Fri 5pm–1am,
Sat–Sun 4pm–1am
Koenji station
[MAP p. 209 A2]

Dizz is a warm, friendly izakaya set in a charming early-20th-century building on Koenji's Central Road. Paper lanterns swing outside and the character continues into the building where vintage Japanese posters seem to keep the walls glued together and kanji menus dangle over a bustling bar. There are many small dishes on offer and the usual extensive izakaya drinks list, but the tasty grilled meat and vegetable skewers are the real star here, especially the chicken with shiso (a type of mint) leaves. Stuffing your face will only set you back ¥2500 or so. Dizz is a great place to eat like a local, and the young Koenjiites tending the bar make it a lively spot to see the precinct in action at night.

7 COFFEE HOUƒE POEM

4-44-5 Koenjiminami, Suginami
3325 1126
nikkahan.co.jp
Open Mon–Sun 11am–9.30pm
[MAP p. 209 B2]

Established in 1961, Poem is more 'beat' than haiku – more Kerouac and Murakami than Basho, bohemian – not barista. A charming vintage yellow sign leads you into a small space where a youthful staff bring an edgy update to the classic, old-school Japanese coffee house. Pork pie hats, tattoos, Zeppelin or Dylan T-shirts and pencil and pad are recommended accessories. The tables have coffee beans layered under the glass tabletops and well-worn benches line the walls in mustard and brown, furniture with stories to tell. Peace and love are still on the menu, along with cheese toast, chiffon cake, hashed beef and rice, and an extensive range of tempting scones. The coffee is classic pour-over, the soundtrack rock and roll, blues and soul. Grab a table and scribble away the afternoon, perhaps composing an ode to the charm of this popular Koenji afternoon hangout.

KICHIJOJI

Perched on the edge of Inokashira Park, this residential neighbourhood has a very local feel. It's the perfect antidote to the madness of the big city and only 20 minutes from Shibuya by express train. You can choose your own adventure here: ride a bicycle down Nakamichi Dori to check out the independent handmade stores; have dinner and drinks in the tiny bars and eateries of Harmonica Yokocho; or stroll down the covered lanes of the Sun Road Arcade.

A picnic in Inokashira Park in sakura (cherry blossom) season makes for the perfect day. Cruise the park's lake in the swan boats or stop off at the Ghibli Museum, a mecca for animation fans.

→ *Inokashira Park's Benzaiten Temple*

1 INOKAƧHIRA PARK

1-18-31 Gotenyama, Musashino
422 47 6900
city.musashino.lg.jp
Open 24-hours
Kichijoji station, park exit,
south gate
[MAP p. 208 A3, C3]

Inokashira Park is one of Tokyo's premium sakura (cherry blossom) viewing spots, a spacious green cocoon where blossoms canopy over the banks of the lake, and couples in swan boats canoodle in private (although local superstition says that that if you do this, a breakup is imminent). Opened in 1918, a gift from the emperor to the public, the park boasts impressive Red Pines, cypress, azaleas and the **Benzaiten Temple**. It hosts some of Tokyo's best festivals – the **Kichijoji Music Festival** (start of April) and the **Kichijoji Anime Festival** (October), which includes the Forest Movie theatre.

The popular **Ghibli Museum** is an organic, mystical toybox. Opened in 2001, the museum is a crusade for anime fans wanting to live inside Ghibli's vision. A world awaits of billowing floaty clouds, giants, robots and children finding their way through a harsh world with the help of plump, soft, creatures who are deeply kind and strangely dark.

POCKET TIP
If you're shopping in Kichijoji check out Markus for exquisite handcrafted goods, Bondo for ceramics and Petit Mura Cat cafe for a drink and a fluffy friend.

2 NAKAMICHI DORI SHOPPING

Kichijoji station, west gate
[MAP p. 208 B1]

Nakamichi Dori is great for a Sunday stroll … especially if you're into shopping. Creative handcraft stores, inspired fashion designers and dedicated vintage collectors make it one of Kichijoji's prime destinations. A few of our favourites on this street are **Wickie**, **Paper Message**, **Avril** and **Hara Donuts** (see p. 129) – but there's plenty more to get excited about.

If you're looking to send parcels or letters, head to **Pack Mart**, an old-fashioned stationery store brimming with postage bags, tapes and things that tie, wrap and bundle. The charming blue-striped exterior of **Coeur de Coeur** will draw you into this shop that sells cute stationery and new and vintage homewares. **Poool 02** makes chic womenswear, beautiful linen pieces in timeless designs. Up a steep flight of stairs is **Free Design**, a small space crammed with international and local homewares and novelties. And that's just the tip of the iceberg. It pays to take your time and really savour this street; you never know what you'll uncover.

POCKET TIP

Vegan-friendly Mamezo make the most delicious Japanese curry.

125

3 ʃUN ROAD ARCADE & HARMONICA YOKOCHO

Kichijoji station, north exit [MAP p. 208 C2]

From the north exit of the station, walk the Sun Road, a covered arcade of concentrated local shopping. The stores are open to the street, providing a vibrant market atmosphere. Meat shop **Satou** sells a grilled minced meat snack that is hugely popular with locals and visitors; the shop's ever-present queue winds past the premium tea and pickle shops, clothing and shoe shops, opticians and pharmacists

Don't miss Harmonica Yokocho, located to the left of the Sun Road Arcade's entrance. This small rabbit warren of restaurants and bars harks back to Tokyo's past, and is a great place to visit at night. Squeeze yourself into a tiny bar here or soak up the atmosphere of bygone Japan in a specialist eatery.

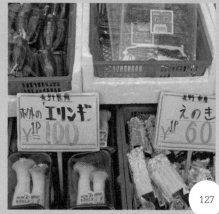

4 I*EYA YAKITORI

1-2-1 Gotenyama,
Musashino-shi
0422 471 008
Open Mon & Wed–Sun
12pm–10pm
Kichijoji station, Park exit
[MAP p. 208 B2]

Nearly 100 years old, this yakitori (grilled skewered meat) joint, housed in a beautiful old building on the way to Inokashira Park, is the real deal. Its old-world frontage and smoke billowing from the chimney make it easy to spot. Join the locals outside and grab some skewers and a beer at the standing bar, or head inside with students and salarymen on a budget to shared tables or tatami rooms. The skewers are mostly pork and the cost is meagre for each. The lunch set is also cheap and cheerful. Be sure to also try the huge shumai (chunky pork dumpling), especially good when washed down with a cold beer. Most importantly, sit back and relax as the kitchen chars another round of pork skewers. Downstairs gets pretty smoky, so if you like your air a bit cleaner, it's probably best to opt for the upstairs room.

POCKET TIP
Stationery lovers should not miss Yamada Stationery in nearby Mitaka.

5 HARA DONUT**S**

4-13-15 Kichijoji Honcho,
Musashino-shi
0422 220 821
Open Mon–Sun 10am–7pm
Kichijoji station, north exit
[MAP p. 208 A1]

You'll have to head to the
end of Nakamichi Dori to
find the stylishly rustic white
frontage of Hara Donuts, but
it's well worth the trip. A
Hara doughnut is not exactly
guilt-free, but compared to a
regular doughnut it sure is.
Made from tofu pulp rather
than dough, these small but
perfectly formed rings are
described by the shop as 'the
way mum used to make them',
although if anyone had a mum
who made doughnuts like this,
lucky them. There are more
than 80 flavours, but we still
managed to find a favourite
(the white chocolate), and each
they're also a bargain. They are
also nuggety little treats that
will fit the bill for any doughnut
craving and may even put you
on the path to righteousness.

POCKET TIP
Nab a delicious
brew from Light Up
Coffee next door.

SHIMOKITAZAWA

Attempts by chain stores and high-rise developers to muscle in on Shimokitazawa's flea-market charm have largely failed, and consequently this breezy precinct is one of Tokyo's most alluring bohemian enclaves. Shimokita, as the locals call it, has a bit of a hippie element.

Endearingly helter-skelter streets and alleys are home to wafer-thin low-rise buildings with offbeat bars, unique record stores, miniscule craft galleries and cafes that do modern spins on Japanese staples. Young Tokyoites scour racks at overstuffed thrift stores, relax at effortlessly cool cafes or seat themselves at bars that look like they've grown overnight in shoebox-sized rooms.

→ *One of Shimokitazawa's indie vintage stores*

/HOPPING
1. Haight & Ashbury
2. Jet Set Records
3. Fog Linen Work

/HOPPING & EATING
4. Darwin Room
5. City Country City

EATING & DRINKING
6. Noumin Organic Cafe
7. Bio Ojiyan Cafe
8. Dashin Soan Soba

1 HAIGHT &
ASHBURY

2-37-2 Kitazawa, Setagaya-ku
5453 4690
haightandashbury.com
Open Mon—Sun 12pm—10pm
Shimokitazawa station,
south exit
[MAP p. 198 B1]

Vintage-clothes shopping is
a sport in Shimokitazawa and
there's no shortage of stores
catering to the fanatical retro
hunter. A case in point is
Haight & Ashbury, a rabbit
warren of a store that's been
perfecting its item hunting
for 20 years. As the San
Francisco—inspired, flower-
power name suggests, there
are a lot of '60s summery florals
and cult lace dresses for sale
here, but last-century European
styles are also well represented,
as are other Americana clothes.
Look for the big red shoe
outside and head on in; you
won't be wading through flea-
bitten cast-offs here. This is a
tasteful selection hand-picked
by people who love their job
and all things yesteryear.

2 JET SET RECORDS

2-33-12 Kitazawa, Setagaya-ku
5452 2262
jetsetrecords.net
Open Mon–Sun 2–10pm
Shimokitazawa station,
south exit
[MAP p. 198 C1]

Hidden away in a nondescript building, this record store is a mecca for house and techno DJs, as well as a regular shopping haunt for anyone obsessed with independent music. The collection is crammed into every nook and cranny, only leaving room for a listening station with a couple of turntables where you can try before you buy. For the claustrophobic, there's a very comprehensive online store, but you don't want to miss the atmosphere here, which harks back to the good ol' days of hunting through your favourite store for the latest vinyl releases. So have a scout around; you're sure to find something interesting, challenging or even life-changing amongst the impressive selection.

133

3 FOG LINEN WORK

5-35-1 Daita, Setagaya-ku
5432 5610
foglinenwork.com
Open Mon–Fri 12pm–6pm
Shimokitazawa station, west exit
[MAP p. 198 A2]

The philosophy at Fog Linen Work is simple: owner Yumiko Sekine believes in creating and selling divine products for daily use. Ten years in the making, this stylish minimalist store converts linen sourced from Lithuania into beautiful and covetable tea towels, bedding, coasters, cushions and a range of dresses and aprons. All items come in simple and tasteful earth tones, or the store's signature checks and stripes. You'll find well-heeled Shimokitazawa residents shopping here, looking for ways to add a touch of class to their homes. Make sure you plan your visit to Fog Linen Work: it's closed on weekends, which is almost unheard of in Tokyo.

4 DARWIN ROOM

5-31-8 Daizawa, Setagaya-ku
6805 2638
Open Mon–Fri 12pm–8pm,
Sat–Sun 12pm–10pm
Shimokitazawa station,
south exit
[MAP p. 198 B3]

Join Darwin on his voyage
of evolutionary discovery
at this quirky cafe with
an impressively verdant
exterior. Victorian-era science
paraphernalia and antiquities
stuff the shelves inside, and
the eyes of hapless taxidermy
victims follow you around
the room. A self-proclaimed
'Liberal Arts Lab', the Darwin
Room has the feel of a museum
or library where scientists of
bygone days scribbled detailed
drawings of moths or orchids.
Mind-bending science books
are for sale, as are curios like
ore samples and pendants with
insects set in acrylic. Enjoy tea
or coffee with cake while you
consider buying a replica skull
of Peking Man.

5 CITY COUNTRY CITY

4F, Hosozawa building, 2-12-13
Shimokitazawa, Setagaya-ku
3410 6080
Open Mon–Tues & Thurs–Fri
12pm–1am, Sat–Sun 11am–1am
Shimokitazawa station,
south exit
[MAP p.198 C2]

Seek out the tiny street sign and take the wobbly lift up four floors to emerge into this pocket-sized cafe and vintage-vinyl store. Owner Keiichi Sokabe was the lead singer of Japanese '90s cult indie band Sunny Day Service, and his love of music shines through in the selection of pre-loved world music, disco, indie-rock, house and space-funk records for sale. Photos of DJs and band autographs on the wall hint that there are good finds here, and Sokabe makes regular international trips to forage for quality records. Sip a latte or a cold beer while enjoying the tunes, or come for the simple and tasty pasta lunch (very inexpensive with tea, coffee or juice usually included). City Country City morphs into a cool bar after dark.

6 NOUMIN ORGANIC CAFE

2-27-8 Kitazawa, Setagaya
5734 1190
livemedia.co.jp/wwc/nong/
about_xue_da.html
Open Mon–Sun 11am–11pm
Shimokitazawa station,
north exit
[MAP p. 198 B1]

Home to '70s retro hippie chic where flares never went out of fashion, a vintage shopping mecca with a relaxed weekend atmosphere, Shimokita is the perfect place for an organic cafe. Rustic, with roots, shoots and legumes of all varieties, plus a mish-mash of retro furniture and Japanese chic, Noumin is a must stop for anyone wanting their food freshly picked and simply prepared. It is housed in a beautiful old backstreet building with a picturesque take-out window for rice and vegetable picnic food. Inside, you can sit cross-legged at low tables and taste food the way it's meant to be – earthy, natural and full of flavour. In the small outside area you can enjoy the fruits of a farmer's labours while looking at the Buddah statue and listening to the sounds of running water and the plucking of koto strings. Lunch set platters are seasonal, fresh and unadorned – rice and meat or fish dishes with tofu, salad, vegetable dishes, quiche and rice.

137

7 BIO OJIYAN CAFE

5-35-25 Shimokitazawa,
Setagaya-ku
5486 6997
Open Mon–Sun 11.30am–11pm
Shimokitazawa station, west exit
[MAP p. 198 B2]

This local and cosy Shimokita cafe specialises in ojiya, a congee-like savoury rice porridge that's the closest thing you'll get to Japanese comfort food. It's also one of the most versatile dishes you'll come across – it goes well with toast soldiers and egg, and meat, fish or vegetables, plus it's great for breakfast, lunch or dinner. The nori (seaweed) and sugar-dusted toast might seem unusual accompaniments, but any doubts will soon be assuaged as you dig into a bowl of this heavenly stodge. Pair it with an iced coffee in summer or a steaming matcha (green tea) latte in winter. The student, artist and vintage-kid clientele here makes for an interesting scene.

8 DASHIN SOAN SOBA

3-7-14 Daizawa, Setagaya-ku
5431 0141
Open Mon–Fri 11.30am–3pm
& 5.30–9.30pm, Sat–Sun
11.30am–9.30pm
Shimokitazawa station,
south exit
[MAP p. 198 C4]

We'll resist the urge to say
'dash in' to this soba-noodle
restaurant, but definitely make
it one of your Shimokitazawa
must-dos. It's a bit of a hike
from the station, but hey,
Tokyo is not a place to stick
to the main roads. Dashin
Soan's charming traditional
entry reveals a restaurant that
raises the national noodle to
an art form. Get stuck into
some classic chilled soba with
dipping sauce or chewy soba
in a hot broth. Our pick is
the duck soba, tender slices
of duck in a steaming golden
soup. As with all good soba
restaurants, staff will bring you
the cooking water to drink, a
cloudy, nourishing broth that
will be unlike anything you've
had before.

POCKET TIP
Weekend vintage
shopping and people-
watching in Shimokita
is a Tokyo must!

139

EBISU, DAIKANYAMA & NAKAMEGURO

Ebisu, Daikanyama and Nakameguro will give you a snapshot of Tokyo at a quieter pace, where the locals go to brunch and 'weekend' and they're all within 15-minutes' walk of each other. Ebisu is a precinct divided. It's a shopping and business district by day, but the real Ebisu gets out of bed at 3pm, pulls on its jeans and opens a beer before heading out for an all-night party. Come evening, roller doors unveil tiny bars, eateries and night cafes. The beer is good, of course, as Ebisu is the home of Yebisu, one of the best Japanese beer brands. Evisu jeans also originate here and are the perfect metaphor for this quirky, inventive and laid-back precinct.

Daikanyama has French pastry shops and high-end fashion boutiques, bringing a feeling of luxe to this quiet precinct. Fledgling Tokyo designers, vintage and craft stores, and indie galleries ensure it also has street cred. The influx of young Tokyoites on weekends adds to the vibrant scene. Nakameguro is a low-rise bohemian precinct with a famous canal, one of the most festive spots in Tokyo during cherry blossom time. It's fringed with hip places to eat, drink and shop overlooking the water. Strolling along the canal and around the backstreets is an absolute joy.

→ *Nakameguro Canal in sakura (cherry blossom) season*

SIGHTS
1. Tokyo Photographic Art Museum (TOP)
2. The Sato Sakura Museum

SHOPPING
3. Cocca
4. 1LDK
5. P.F.S. Parts Center
6. Traveler's Factory
7. Minä Perhonen
8. Junie Moon
9. T-Site

EATING & DRINKING
10. Tatemichiya
11. Afuri Ramen
12. Ebisu Yokocho
13. Higashi-Yama
14. Mahakala's Happy Pudding
15. Akira

1 TOKYO PHOTOGRAPHIC ART MUSEUM (TOP)

Yebisu Garden Place, 1-13-3
Mita, Meguro-ku
3280 0099
topmuseum.jp
Open Tues–Sun 10am–6pm
[MAP p. 201 D2]

Established in 1986, a 2016 refurbishment took the Tokyo Photographic Art Museum (or TOP, as it is known) from a brilliant photography museum to one of the world's best. Walking towards the gallery is an experience in itself, with huge photographs on the walls setting the scene. The museum has collected its own works over the years amassing some truly special contemporary pieces, both Japanese and from around the world. Three galleries show edgy contemporary works, classic photographic portfolios and international showcases, often with political and social undertones. A visit to the gallery at any time will be informative, challenging and enlightening. One of the highlights is a free reference library stocking an amazing range of Japanese and international books on the art of the camera that any photography buff should take full advantage of.

2 THE SATO SAKURA MUSEUM

1-7-13 Kamimeguro, Meguro
3496 1771
satosakura.jp
Open Tues–Sun 10am–6pm
Nakameguro station
[MAP p. 200 B2]

As one of the prime spots for sakura (cherry blossom) viewing, Nakameguro's pink-washed canal is the perfect place for a museum that celebrates all things sakura. The museum's exterior is an all-black towering slab of marble with etched cherry blossoms, a wall of flowers creating an entrance where you can slip into a world devoted to the worshipped flower. The museum is primarily concerned with 'contemporary Nihonga', a style of painting made famous in the Showa period, essentially a rebirth of traditional Japanese painting made to offset the growing popularity of 'Yoga', a very western style. Nihonga is perfect for sakura – flowers, leaves, fruit, branches, cats and people in traditional dress are cast in a dreamlike, beautiful world. A trip to Nakameguro during sakura isn't complete without visiting this museum.

POCKET TIP
Visit the beautiful newly opened Arts & Science store in Daikanyama.

143

3 COCCA

1-31-13 Ebisunishi, Shibuyaku
3463 7681
Open Tues–Sun 11am–9pm
Daikanyama station
[MAP p. 200 C1]

Just off the main drag, Cocca's white modernist building sits among a flourishing garden in a semi-residential part of Ebisu. When you enter it's like you've been invited into someone's home to see their immaculate textile collection, which the streamlined interior allows to speak for itself. The emphasis here is on nurturing new talent, and the expertise of local artisans is truly on display. You'll find intricate handmade fabrics (the heavy linen is exquisite), and designs that are bold and contemporary, or abstract updates on traditional motifs. Dressmakers can grab armfuls of material, while crafters can get hold of handy small offcuts. Cocca's mission statement is to drape everything in fabric, and after you've dropped by you'll definitely want to wrap yourself and your house in these beautiful textiles.

Inspiration of Fabric by

POCKET TIP
Pop into Allegory Home Tools across the road after your fabric fix.

COCCa

4 1LDK

1-8-28 Kamimeguro,
Meguro-ku
3780 1645
Open Mon–Sun 10am–5pm
Nakameguro station
[MAP p. 200 B2]

Away from the canal in
residential Nakameguro,
1LDK is making its own scene
with an effortlessly cool men's
fashion concept store that has
all the locals talking. Owner
Takayuki Minami is here to
make your every day, well, less
everyday with a range of up-
to-the-minute men's clothing,
accessories, stationery,
glasses and whatever else he
deems worthy. (Incidentally,
this is the best selection of
men's spectacles we've seen
in Tokyo.) The stylish store
retains its original look and
feel, as does its older sibling
across the street, **Taste and
Sense**, which sells mostly
womenswear and homewares,
and has an excellent
cafe and bookstore.

5 P.F.S. PARTS CENTER

1-17-5 Ebisu-Minami,
Shibuyaku
3719 8935
pfservice.co.jp
Open Wed–Mon 11am–8pm
Ebisu station
[MAP p. 201 D2]

A retro mishmash of an army surplus and classic hardware store, P.F.S Parts Center will have the DIY enthusiast drooling and the weekend camper stocking up on tin plates, spoons, forks, sporks and anything else needed for the great outdoors. Items are perfect for travelling in the great indoors as well. Industrial lighting, filing cabinets, tools, door knobs, screws, cables, latches and handles are all represented in this knockabout selection of handyman essentials and everyday fundamentals. As a traveller, this is a great place to stock up on quality and classic bits and bobs; we posted a mailbox back home. There's nothing quite like the vintage take on everyday items here. The oddball selection of garden variety knick-knacks make P.F.S. Parts Center an inspirational fossick for both the amateur and professional jack of all trades.

POCKET TIP
The streets around P.F.S Parts Center showcase some of Tokyo's most interesting architecture.

146

6 TRAVELER'S FACTORY

3-13-10, Kamimeguro,
Meguro-ku
6412 7830
travelers-factory.com
Open Mon 12pm–8pm,
Wed–Sun 12pm–8pm
Nakameguro station, west exit
[MAP p. 200 B2]

More than one pilgrimage
has been made to this tiny
store to bow down to the
gods of stationery. Set up in
2006, Traveler's Factory is the
home of Traveler's Notebook,
a cult journal. If you're into
bullet-point journaling, or
keeping a travel diary, buy
the Notebook, then customise
it with a range of quirky and
retro additions. Once inside
it's wall-to-wall journal junkies
as the building, like your
notebook, is pocket-sized.
Vintage-style stamps, pockets,
pouches, covers, bags, brass
fountain pens, sharpeners and
cases are all much-needed
extras. Light rainwear to shield
your notebook from sudden
downpours, is made to fold
neatly into your bag. Traveler's
Factory is hidden down an
enclave that even Google
Maps has trouble finding,
you'll see tourists discovering
the meaning of 'intrepid',
looking up and down alleyways
and lanes.

POCKET TIP
Try one of Tokyo's best
Taiyaki (fish-shaped
cake) at Ginza
Taiyaki Sakuraya.

7 MINÄ PERHONEN

Hillside Terrace, GF-1F
102/103, 18-12 Sarugakucho,
Shibuyaku
6826 3770
mina-perhonen.jp/en
Open Mon–Sun 12pm–8pm
Daikanyama station
[MAP p. 200 B1]

Designer Akira Minagawa's
drawings and patterns are
inspired by his passion for
Finland. Indeed, his fashion
and textile brand Minä
Perhonen has its origins in
the Finnish language: 'minä'
means 'I' and 'perhonen'
is 'butterfly'. As such,
Minagawa's designs, as much
art as they are fashion, mimic
the delicate and timeless
beauty of a butterfly's wing.
The brand is well known and
coveted by anyone into fabric
creation, print techniques,
meticulous and intricate
textiles. Float through the shop;
its warm woods, soft lights
and always inspiring displays
make it the perfect showcase
for the beautiful clothes. This
Minä Perhonen clothing store
is the flagship (or visit the Call
store in Aoyama and Piece
in Harajuku).

8 JUNIE MOON

1F, Suzuen Daikanyama
Building, 4-3 Sarugakucho,
Shibuyaku
juniemoon.jp
Open Tues–Sun 11am–9pm
Daikanyama station
[MAP p. 200 C1]

Blythe is a fashion doll like
no other. Her oversized head,
massive eyes, super cuteness
and to-die-for wardrobe have
spawned an army of obsessive
collectors. Junie Moon is a
mecca for Blythe's many fans
and serves as a catwalk for
the much-loved doll to rock
her latest styles. You can
spend hours here hunting
through brightly coloured
boxes for vintage 'skate
date' or 'bohemian beats'
outfits for your dolly, or you
can catch up on the latest-
release Blythe models, one-offs
and exclusives. The store
even hosts 'Salon de Junie
Moon', a monthly workshop
with hands-on instructions
for how to make your own
Blythe outfits. Devotees will
also want to stock up on
stationery, tote bags and
other Blythe-related items.
It's almost impossible not to
smile along with the young,
over-excited clientele.

149

EBISU, DAIKANYAMA &
NAKAMEGURO

9 T-SITE

17-5 Sarugakucho, Shibuyaku
3770 2525
Open Mon–Sun 7am–2am
Daikanyama station
[MAP p. 200 B1]

So much more than a
bookstore, this biosphere
dedicated to all things
peruse-worthy has become
a magnet for bibliophiles
and weekend browsers
alike. T-Site has an absurdly
extensive range of books of
every genre, including a large
selection of English releases.
One of the big drawcards
is 'Magazine Street', which
boasts around 30,000 vintage
magazines (mostly from the
'60s and '70s), as well as the
latest publications.

T-Site also stocks well over
100,000 CDs and DVDs (staff
will even burn previously
unavailable classics to disc for
you!). Awesome workstations
and reading sections turn the
landmark building into a mini
library, and on the second floor
you can leaf through a book
at the excellent cafe **Anjin**.
And that's not all folks! Within
the grounds there's a camera
store with a **Leica museum**,
a dog-grooming salon and **Ivy
Place**, a hugely popular cafe
and bar. You could easily lose a
day in this mega-complex, and
on Sundays hordes of Tokyoites
do just that.

POCKET TIP
Café Red Book is a
cosy back street curry
house in Nakameguro,
great for a quick
lunch or dinner after
a day's shopping.

10 TATEMICHIYA

B1F, 30-8 Sarugakucho,
Shibuyaku
5459 3431
Open Mon–Fri 6pm–4am,
Sat–Sun 6pm–12am
Daikanyama station
[MAP p. 200 C1]

Hey ho, let's go! The fun
kicks off at night in this
grungy izakaya, a magnet for
provocative, art-conscious
locals, hang-abouts and rock
'n' roll diehards. Expect posters
of the Sex Pistols and Ramones
and a soundtrack of punk,
rock and punk rock, turned
up to 11. Pop artist Yoshitomo
Nara loves it here; check out
his handiwork on the walls at
the back and Mick Jagger's
signature on the front wall
near the entrance. The honest
izakaya fare includes delicious
grilled skewers of meat, and
atsuage (deep-fried tofu) that
people cross town for. Be brave
and add some natto (fermented
soybeans) to your meal; you'll
either hate or handle this
stinky bean. Your host will be
cheerfully singing along to the
music while pouring your sake.
Tatemichiya is unpretentious
and its food delicious, and as a
result Daikanyama's cool kids
and faded rockers come here
in droves.

EBISU, DAIKANYAMA &
NAKAMEGURO

11 AFURI RAMEN

1-1-7 Ebisu, Shibuyaku
5795 0750
afuri.com
Open Mon–Sun 11am–5pm
Ebisu station, east exit
[MAP p. 201 D1]

This ramen joint selling
wonderful, intensely flavoured
noodle soups is just a hop,
skip and a jump from Ebisu
station. It's in-and-out dining –
no lingering here! – so slip
some money into the vending
machine to order your meal on
the way in (there's an English
menu), pick your ramen,
choose your noodle type and
grab a seat at the counter. You
can customise your dish if you
like; we recommend adding
extra crispy nori sheets. If you
find ramen a bit heavy, get
the speciality, the delicious
yuzu broth; this citrus fruit
creates a light and tangy dish
that will leave you wanting
more. For those of you who
don't eat pork, the broth is
made of chicken and you can
ask for it without pork slices.
They also do a seasonal vegan
ramen. Whatever you end up
ordering, take a cue from your
neighbours and slurp it to your
heart's content.

EBISU-YOKOCHO

POCKET TIP
In an almost hidden store, Yaeca's clothes are the height of understated everyday style.

12 EBISU YOKOCHO

1-17-4 Ebisu-Minami,
Shibuyaku
6268-8799
ebisu-yokocho.com
Open Sun–Mon 5pm–5am
Ebisu station
[MAP p. 201 D1]

At night Ebisu comes alive, grills start to sizzle and smoke as roller doors reveal secret, hidden canteens and coffee shops, workers flood into the area and the station hub is abuzz with feverish activity as commuters seek to appease their hunger. Ebisu Yokocho is the distilling of that mad magic – a market space of separate eateries (and drinkeries) where you can find an array of food in tiny hawker bars all elbow to elbow in one central space. With a 5am closing time you can tell that Ebisu Yokocho was made for good, messy times. This was the place where the old Yamashita 'shopping center' used to thrive, a relic of days gone by, now it is a mish-mash of Japanese-, Chinese- and even French-style bars and eateries. You can mix it up with locals and visitors until, bleary eyed, you find yourself staggering through the streets of Ebisu with the street sweepers and early risers for company …

153

13 HIGAʃHI-YAMA

1-21-25 Higashiyama, Meguro
5720 1300
higashiyama-tokyo.jp
Open Mon 6pm–12am,
Tues–Sat 11.30am–3pm &
6pm–12am
Nakameguro station
[MAP p. 200 A1]

Washoku is essentially 'traditional Japanese food,' and if you want to see it elevated to an art form, Higashi-yama is the place to be. Design company Simplicity has put its know-how into both the space and the food. Gather your friends together – Higashi-yama's washoku is a dish best served communal, so everyone can comment on the exquisite decor, the delicious fare, the flowing regional sake and the 'I-need-that-in-my-house-right-now' ceramics and utensils. The dining space is beautiful at night when low lighting and warm woods are highlighted and by day the communal tables and counter dining make for an intimate experience. The bento are served in truly exquisite wood boxes. Its *tres* cool design and fashion-conscious locals, referred to as 'tarento' (the talent), are regular customers. Try the delicious wagu beef cutlet, zaru-dofu, melt-in-the-mouth squid or fish and seasonal vegetables like white asparagus or a green tea panna cotta for dessert.

POCKET TIP

Nakameguro is a good spot for pizza, try Da Isa, Seirinkan and Baird beer, and for coffee Onibus and Jaho Coffee.

14 MAHAKALA'S HAPPY PUDDING

1-17-5, Aoba Maison 101,
Aobadai, Meguro-ku
6427 8706
Open Mon–Sun 11am–6pm
Nakameguro station
[MAP p. 200 B1]

This hole-in-the-wall spot on a street along the canal sells glorious hits of creamy egg custard that come in tiny glass pots. The flavours range from the delicious classic caramel to the equally good matcha, a green-tea custard for those who like their sweets a little less sweet but with a whole lot of interesting. Then there's the black sesame, the honey lemon, the chestnut chocolate pudding, the tiramisu … oh excuse me, I just went to pudding heaven in my mind … If you can't decide what to choose, look for the number one on the menu (which indicates the best-selling item). Whatever you pick, you can't go wrong for taste or value. Staff politely request that you recycle the takeaway pots, but taking them home and using them as vases is the same thing, right?

15 AKIRA

1-10-23 Nakameguro,
Meguro-ku
3793 0051
Open Mon–Sun 5pm–3am
Nakameguro station
[MAP p. 200 B2]

If you're looking for one of
the best izakaya experiences
in Tokyo, Akira will fit the
brief. A hidden gem, it's in a
stunning old-school building
at the end of a tiny strip
overlooking the canal. The
interior is beautiful, traditional
and rustic, and the scent of
smoke and grilled meats wafts
over you on arrival. It's great
fun grilling your own meat at
your table, but the chicken
tartare in ponzu (a citrus-
based sauce) is what most
people come here for. We also
recommend the fried chicken
skin, which is as delicious and
wonderfully bad for you as it
sounds. Make sure you book,
as it's deservedly popular and
gets busy quickly, especially on
weekends. Pull up a cushion on
the bamboo floor for the best
views, then sit back with a
draught beer or a plum wine.

IN & AROUND MEGURO

Fondly known as 'interior street' for its abundance of furniture and homewares stores, sweeping Meguro Dori links the two creative precincts of Gakugei-daigaku and Meguro. To the north-east of bustling Meguro station you'll find parks, gardens, teahouses and in-the-know shopping opportunities. West of the station, there's a covered arcade crammed with pocket-sized old-world eateries, while hip new bars and coffee houses are sprouting around the river.

Gakugei-daigaku has much more of a residential neighbourhood feel, with plenty of quaint restaurants and great little shopping finds amongst its patchwork of tiny streets.

→ Floristry – Meguro style

SIGHTS
1. Tokyo Metropolitan Teien Art Museum
2. Meguro Parasitological Museum

SHOPPING
3. Meguro Dori (Interior Street)

SHOPPING & EATING
4. Geographica
5. Chum Apartment
6. Claska Gallery & Cafe

EATING & DRINKING
7. Happo-en
8. Switch Coffee

1 TOKYO METROPOLITAN TEIEN ART MUSEUM

5-21-9 Shirokanedai, Minato
3443 0201
teien-art-museum.ne.jp
Open Mon–Sun 10am–6pm,
opening hours can vary,
check website
Meguro station, east exit
[MAP p. 201 E3]

The former residence of Prince
Asaka, this museum was
reimagined and redesigned by
French architect Henri Rapin.
Completed in 1933, the exterior
is chic European, the interior
lavish Art Deco opulence,
reflected in every doorknob,
archway and fireplace. The
ornate and finely detailed
staircase, tiled floors and
grates alone are worth the visit.
Black and white check hallway
tiles are straight out of a '60's
French film or perhaps *Alice in
Wonderland*. It's a fine example
of a building influenced by
western styles but created
with a Japanese aesthetic.
The exhibitions always sit
well in the space – painting,
design, sculpture, furniture
and decorative objects within
the airy rooms. The building
sits proudly on vast expanses
of perfectly manicured lawns
with strategically placed
modernist sculptures. Nooks
and enclaves have ponds,
water features, a tea house,
stepping stones and bridges all
with exquisite planting.

POCKET TIP
If you are a garden
lover visit the amazing
Institute of Nature
Study Shizenkyoikuen
next door.

POCKET TIP
Teien has a lovely cafe
overlooking the gardens
and a store selling
beautiful wares.

2 MEGURO PARASITOLOGICAL MUSEUM

4-1-1 Shimomeguro, Meguro
3716 1264 (recorded
information in Japanese only)
kiseichu.org/e-top
Open Thurs–Sun 10am–5pm
Meguro station, west exit
[MAP p. 200 C4]

In a world of mergers and
take-overs who knew all this
activity could be happening
in your own body? Small yet
extremely effective, parasites
make it their life goal to invade
and conquer. The museum was
founded in 1953, a scientific
facility that plays 'host' to
50,000 scientific papers and
5000 books, plus an almost
nine-metre tapeworm, who
infected his human after he ate
a fish supper. As a curiosity,
it's certainly one of the world's
most informative and inventive
museums. As a science facility
the research is invaluable and
up-to-the minute – although it
might be the hatching ground
for a new species that will take
over the world. The sci-curious
will love assorted tanks and
containers showcasing a range
of parasites. The 'helminths'
(fluke, tapeworm and
roundworm, etc.) all appear
in formaldehyde-filled bottles
and possibly later in your
nightmares – it's all informative
and instructive fun. Don't
forget to pick up a tapeworm
T-shirt on the way out.

3 MEGURO DORI (INTERIOR STREET)

Meguro Dori, Meguro
Gakugei-daigaku or
Meguro station
[MAP p. 200 C4]

A lazy walk from Gakugei-daigaku station brings you to Meguro Dori, aka Interior Street. It has a European feel with a J-twist with vintage-inspired cafes, retro streetlights and furniture restorers. Dogs are dressed better than people. The action happens just before the stylish Claska Hotel and stretches down to the Otori Shrine. **Case Study Store** has mid-century and 1950's kitsch (they also invented a Cover-It-All for the Eames Eiffel DAW Chair), **Otsu** specialises in Japanese antiques and curios; **Linus** has cute knick-knacks and craft to adorn your home; **Sonechika** is known for high-end mid-century; **Junks** has Americana; and **Blackboard** excels in industrial. Stores like **Acme** and **Karf** are a modern take on vintage. Stop for lunch at the dark and moody **Antique Café** or head just off the main drag to find the wave-like noodle strands that adorn the exterior of soba eatery **Yufutoku**. You can even get an old-school shave at **Ishioka Salon**.

POCKET TIP
Book and Sons has an incredible range of vintage typography books.

椅子張替
(03)3792-1950

4 GEOGRAPHICA

1-25-20 Naka, Meguro
5773 1145
geographica.jp
Open Mon–Sun 11am–8pm
Gakugei-daigaku station,
east exit
[MAP p. 200 B4]

If you love sifting through antiques, oddments and ephemera from days gone by, Geographica's three storeys of antique whimsy will be your idea of a great day out. Mahogany and walnut furniture, lace bonnets, teddy bears and shelves of fine china sit alongside pre-loved European and Japanese books, matchboxes, magazines and badges from the '50s and '60s. Have a leaf through the old postcards: you never know, you might recognise a distant relative. Locals and those who speak Japanese can take furniture restoration classes in the Geographica workshop. On the second floor there's **Il Levante**, a gorgeous little Italian cafe set out like train compartments where you can take a break from all that rummaging.

5 CHUM APARTMENT

2-23-3 Shimomeguro, Meguro
3490 2921
Open Mon–Sat 12pm–12am,
Sun 12pm–6pm (bar and cafe);
Mon–Sun 12pm–8pm (shop)
Meguro station, west exit
[MAP p. 201 D4]

Japanese artist Chiharu
Yoshikawa took a run-down
mansion on a quiet Meguro
backstreet and turned it
into local hot spot Chum
(pronounced 'charm')
Apartment. Look for the
Kombi-like van parked out
the front, a hint of the hippie
traveller vibe that extends to
the Moroccan colour palette
inside this cafe-cum-bar-cum-
shop. The peeling discoloured
walls, iron latticework, crosses,
skulls and low-lit chandeliers
give the place an eerie feel,
but the repurposed furniture
and deep couches cosy things
up. Grab a daily set lunch
for around ¥1100, including
coffee or tea, then head up to
Mucha on the second floor, a
shop selling rustic handmade
ceramics. It's open late, so
come back at night, slip into
one of the nooks and crannies
in the cafe-bar, order a wine,
beer or shochu (distilled spirit)
and make like a local.

POCKET TIP
Don't miss the
secluded Meguro
Museum of Art.

6 CLAƧKA GALLERY & CAFE

1-3-18 Chuocho, Meguro
3719 8123
claska.com
Open Mon–Sun 11am–7pm
(shop and gallery);
7.30am–12am (cafe)
Gakugei-daigaku station,
east exit
[MAP p. 200 A4]

It's a bit of a walk from the station, but Claska is one of Tokyo's, if not the world's, best boutique hotels. It's ultra stylish and yet unpretentious, a feat made possible by supreme attention to detail combined with friendly staff. If you don't happen to be staying here, there's still every reason to visit. Gallery shop **Do** is a sublimely curated selection of new Japanese design, craft and everyday items that you'll no doubt want to take home with you. Attached is a small gallery that shows regular exhibitions by local designers and illustrators. Cafe/restaurant **Kiokuh** is one of the city's coolest places to hang out. The pick of the menu is the Japanese breakfast, but it's also the perfect place for evening drinks or an afternoon coffee and cake while you watch pooches being pampered at the adjacent canine spa **Dogman**.

7 HAPPO-EN

1-1-1 Shirokanedai, Minato-ku
3443 3775
happo-en.com
Open Fri–Tues 11am–6pm
Shirokanedai station, exit 2
[MAP p. 201 F3]

Happo-en means 'garden of eight views', and the wonders of this garden are indeed truly stunning from any angle. Water features, rockeries and a beautiful display of bonsai, some ranging from 200 to 500 years old, are just some of the delights in this peaceful oasis tucked away amid the broad streets and bustling traffic of Meguro. The main building is worth a look (as the faint '70s style is kind of cool), but the main attraction is the tea ceremony in the front room of a Meiji-era house, where you can order a light meal of delicious green tea and sweets, or go for the full experience. If you're in the market for something special, splash out and take the Edo Romance garden walk, a tour of the garden complete with tea ceremony and dinner in the restaurant.

8 **SWITCH COFFEE**

1-17-23 Meguro, Meguro-ku
6420 3633
switchcoffeetokyo.com
Open Mon–Sun 10am–7pm
Meguro station, west exit
[MAP p. 201 D3]

This hole-in-the-wall coffee stand is off the main strip but it's well worth the wander. Everything about the place is done well; the exterior is stylish, and the row of coffee machines along the counter is a deft touch. This is a takeaway kind of joint, with no seats, but you can rest on a small wooden bench outside. Staff here are friendly and knowledgeable; they talk about coffee like it's fine wine, referring to regions, bean varieties and fruit aromas, and might suggest a particular blend has a hint of blueberry jam or an afterglow of sweet brown sugar. If a particular blend takes your fancy, you can buy beans in 250-gram packets to go. Terms like 'single origin' and 'Costa Rican dragon' can make you feel like you're getting your hands on something illicit, and the coffee is so darn good that you may as well be.

POCKET TIP
Old-school eateries line Meguro dori between the station and the river.

167

NIKKO

Nikko is perfect if you're looking for natural beauty, ancient monuments, bridges, lakes, secluded temples, local food and stunning scenery. It is famous for its autumnal foliage and has several impressive sakura (cherry blossom) sites.

If you plan a daytrip, choose your trains carefully as travel times can be long. Once there, buy the Tobu Nikko free pass giving you access to bus travel around Nikko and discounts on some sights. From Nikko station take the bus for Lake Chuzenji stopping at Shinkyo and Nishisando, where you can walk to the temples. The World Heritage Meguri Bus loops around the sights taking in Toshogu Shrine, Rinnoji Temple, Futarasan Shrine and Taiyu-In. The walk takes in some of Japan's best forestry, tumbling waterfalls (Kegon Waterfall drops nearly 100 metres) and stunning Kanmangafuchi Abyss. Chuzenji's lake district has stunning views and onsen (Japanese hot spring bath houses), such as Yumoto, Kotoku and Chuzenji Onsen. Kinugawa Onsen north-east of Nikko station, is a playful spa and holiday resort, or for a more secluded trip head up to the Kirifuri Highlands and visit stunning Kirifuri Falls.

→ *The British Embassy, Lake Chuzenji*

TRAIN ACCE//

The most direct way to get from Tokyo to Nikko is the Tobu train from Asakusa. If you have a JR pass try one of the routes in the map opposite from Tokyo, Shinjuku, Ueno or Ikebukuro. Book tickets and get info at a large train station at least one day before you leave. The fastest trains all have reserved seating.

NIKKO SIGHTS

A vermilion lacquered bridge straddling a raging river sits at the foot of the main temple area. Walk from there up to sumptuous World Heritage UNESCO site, **The Toshogu Shrine**, dedicated to legendary shogun Tokugawa Ieyasu. He clearly wanted to be remembered and constructed an extravagant memorial. The courtyard includes a colourful carving of the **Three Wise Monkeys** and the **Kairo**, an ornate cloister. An impressive gate welcomes you into the mausoleum area and decorative prayer hall. The memorial itself is understated considering all the pomp you encounter along the way, but somehow the grueling trek up endless flights of steps affords Ieyasu the respect he deserves. Nearby **Futasaran Shrine**, is dedicated to Mount Nantai, the god of good luck and marriage. The grounds feature two impressive cedars, forever joined in holy matrimony.

Further afield, **Lake Chuzenji** is simply beautiful. Mid-century gems **Italian Embassy House Memorial Park** and **British Embassy Villa Memorial Park** (*see* p. 171) sit on the edge of the lake. What a posting it must have been, the view across the lake to **Mount Nantai** is stunning.

NIKKO ſHOPPING & EATING

Nikko is famous for vegetarian cuisine, especially zaru soba (noodles with dipping sauce) and yuba (tofu skin), onsen manju (a sweet bun steamed with onsen water and plump with adzuki red bean), shisomaki togarashi (red pepper rolled in shiso leaf) and Shojin Ryori (a feast of small vegetable dishes perfected by Buddhist monks). Japanese beef, pork and freshwater fish are also highly rated. A short walk from Nikko and Tobu Nikko Stations, **Uoyou** makes a delectable soba soup with rolled yuba and a superb zaru soba, (book ahead).

Try the generous portions of soba noodles at hidden gem **Houtoku-an**, next to Kami-Imaichi station. For ¥40–¥60 you can get shojin ryori sets at **Gyoshintei**, near **Toshogu Shrine**. The soft serve ice-cream at the **Nikko Toshogu Museum** is a lifesaver on hot days. Make like a Victorian-era diplomat and have lunch or tea and scones at the **British Embassy Villa Memorial Park** cafe, where you can sit on actual Charles Rennie Mackintosh chairs and gaze out over **Lake Chuzenji**. **Yuzawaya Zaryo** is famous for manju. All local delicacies can be found at street stalls in and around the temples and shrines.

FIELD TRIP

HAKONE

Hakone boasts magnificent views of the inimitable Mt Fuji, country air, hot springs, art, cable cars and even a pirate ship! Throw in easy access from Tokyo and it's no wonder it's one of Tokyo's most popular day trips with locals and tourists. Board the wonderfully named Odakyu Romancecar from Shinjuku station, and be whisked along to Hakone in as little as one hour and fifteen minutes. The name of the train hints that this area is a popular spot for couples wanting a 'weekend away'. Plenty of families, onsen hoppers (Japanese hot spring bath houses) and international visitors make the trip as well, keen to soak up some authentic Japanese countryside. The Odakyu Romancecar stops at Hakone-Yumoto station – the site of a quaint little village with meandering streets, old school snack food sellers and a raging river that surges through the town and provides magnificent views for precariously perched hotels. In recent times, the onsen in Hakone have become some of the country's best and take in both the new and chic (Yuryo) and the old school and atmospheric (Tenzan and Kamon). For a five-star Fuji view, try the Green Plaza Hotel (in Gora). If you want to see Mt Fuji up close and personal, Fujikyu, Keio and Kanto Buses have services to Fuji 5 Lakes from Shinjuku, Tokyo and Shibuya stations.

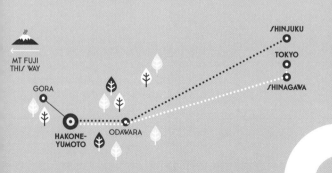

↦ The entrance to Hakone Yuryo

TRAIN ACCESS
If you have a JRail
pass catch the Kodama
Shinkansen from Tokyo
or Shinagawa stations to
Odawara station and then
pay for a local Odakyu
train to Hakone–Yumoto.

173

POCKET TIP

If you want to visit an onsen but are feeling a little shy, Yunessun Hotspring allows swimwear in some areas.

HAKONE SIGHTS

From Hakone-Yumoto station you can ride the sleepy Hakone Tozan 'mountain railway' up to Gora. Stop off at Chokoku-no-Mori station and visit the wonderful **Hakone Open-Air Sculpture Museum**. From Gora get the ropeway across the **Owakudani**, The Great Boiling Valley. The lightly slumbering volcano beneath you steams and smokes through vents in the earth, letting you know that one day it could erupt if it wanted to. It hasn't for thousands of years, so don't hold your breath. Actually do hold your breath, the sulfuric gas can be quite pungent. It's good for cooking those delicious black onsen eggs (*see* p. 175). Once you're at the top, Mount Hakone's peak, **Kami-yama**, overlooks two caldera lakes. **Lake Ashi** is a famous tourist spot featuring **Haiden Hakone Jinja** with its impressive vermilion Tori gate. **Mt Fuji** looms majestically beyond, you can see it from Lake Ashi, the ropeway (on a clear day), the Choanji Temple or various points along Hakone's many walking trails. Mt Fuji can also be enjoyed from sightseeing boats, including three ornate pirate ships. One, the *Vasa*, comes complete with cosplay pirates (yo-ho-ho and a bottle of sake anyone?).

HAKONE SHOPPING & EATING

Hakone has plenty of specialty snacks. Most of them can be nabbed in the main street of old Hakone that winds up from Hakone-Yumato station. Top of the list is the black egg, an onsen tamago with added sulfur. Boiled in the waters of the volcano, it becomes black, salty, healthy and irresistible. **Owakudani Kurotamago kan** on the mountain ropeway stop of Owakudani specialises in onsen black eggs, or you can find them at street vendors. **Manju-Ya Nanohana** makes Onsen manju (sweet buns cooked in the onsen water). To try the area's famous red-snapper rice, visit **Yoraku**. The **Watanabe Bakery**

does an 'onsen stew bread,' a hollowed-out bun with a bubbling, onsen cooked beef stew inside. Hakone's other staple is soba, the best pick here is to have it with the area's famous tofu or grated yam (sweet potato) from **Hatsuhana**. Hakone Beer is an award-winning, semi-craft beer enhanced by the magical waters of the region. If you are looking for a more serious meal dine at one of the area's onsen. For example, **Tenzan**'s stunning building not only hides one of Japan's most rustic hot springs, but has amazing restaurants as well.

MT TAKAO

Fifty minutes and some loose change from Shinjuku station on the Chuo or Keio lines to Takaosanguchi, will deposit you into the heart of a spiritual mountain retreat. The humble mountain station has been given a designer make-over with architect Kengo Kuma forming an impressive structure from the area's spectacular cedar wood. It reflects the shape of the mountain's sacred site, the Yakouin Temple. Walks, beautiful views and peaceful glades are all within easy reach. Catch the funicular railway, or fun, old-school, pop-coloured, chair-lift up the mountain – the vistas of the mountain's greenery and Tokyo's distant metropolis (particularly on the way down) are stunning. Walking is the main pastime on Mt Takao and it's a virtual choose-your-own-adventure of trails. There are Tori gates, statues, impressive trees and views. If you missed cherry blossoms in the main part of Tokyo, you'll be happy to know that they arrive fashionably late to the party on Mt Takao.

MT TAKAO   TAKAO   SHINJUKU

TAKAOSANGUCHI

→ *Entrance to Ukai Toriyama, Mt Takao*

MT TAKAO SIGHTS

The **Yakouin Temple** was founded in 744. It's Japan's third-oldest Buddhist temple and home to a group of aesthetic monks, the **Shugen-do**. Ritual watchers can follow them through the mountains and be transfixed when they sit under the Biwa or Hebi waterfalls and meditate, the water caressing their bald heads, inducing a trance-like state. Preceded by the stunning **Nio-Mon** wooded gate, the grounds of the temple are extensive. The revered crow god Tengu appears in various beaked or bewinged forms around the temple grounds. Outside the shrine, Takao's mountaintop view gives you a chance to take in iconic Mt Fuji and Tokyo's magnificent sprawl. A walk along the mountain includes Tori gates, lanterns, bridges, stone statues, memorial tablets, giant cedars and the **octopus tree** whose root system resembles tentacles. If you want to read up on the mountain, head to the free **Takao 599 Museum** (so named because of the elevation). Amongst all this nature and history, there's a contemporary onsen, the stylish **Keio Takaosan** onsen (*see* p. 179), next to the station. It's perfect to soak aching bones after all that walking.

MT TAKAO SHOPPING & EATING

At the top of Mt Takao you will find restaurants serving dishes with tororo soba (grated sweet potato), the region's specialty. You can enjoy it with beer and some impressive views. In and around the funicular railway and Takaosanguchi station you'll find plenty of snack opportunities, souvenir and street food vendors (including delicious grilled dango) and the area's specialty: a purple soft serve, 'honeyberry' ice-cream made of blueberries and honeysuckle dew. Try the crispy blackbean pastry in the shape of the crow god Tengu. Vegetarians rejoice – book ahead to join the monks in the **Yakouin Temple** (*see* p. 178) for a Shojin Ryori (a feast of small vegetable dishes) banquet. **Ukai Toriyama** is truly special – a shuttle from the station brings you to a wooded glade replete with waterwheels, stone statues, moss and twittering birdlife. You'll be led to your own private tiny hut, before being presented with a visual and culinary feast. If you're heading into **Keio Takaosan** onsen for a soak, you can also eat there, they have a chirpy cafe offering tasty and well-priced lunch sets.

FIELD TRIP

KAMAKURA

Kamakura is a seaside and mountain retreat and 1000 years ago was the centre for Japanese politics, where the Shoguns (and various Regents) ruled over Japan. One of Tokyo's most popular daytrips, Kamakura is less than 40 minutes from the city. It takes you into the heart of the country and boasts a giant Buddha statue, ocean views and incredible cultural sites. It's beautiful in spring when the cherry blossoms are blooming and amazing in summer when the air is kissed by a cool sea breeze and the scent of hydrangeas.

The JR Shonen–Shinjuku line and Yokosuka line or the Odakyu railways will get you there from Tokyo – or depending on your schedule you can try hopping on and off the famous Eno-den. Established on Christmas day 1900, the Eno-den's vintage-style train cars wind in and out of narrow pathways, almost touching houses and roads, delivering chirpy day-trippers to the beachside towns of Enoshima and Kamakura. At under ¥700 the Kamakura–Enoshima pass makes travelling the Eno-den a bargain. From Kamakura station, Komachidori (the main street) is a leisurely stroll towards the Tsurugaoka Hachimangu Shrine. There are many delicious snack shops (mochi, rice crackers etc) and kawaii (cute) souvenir shops along the way.

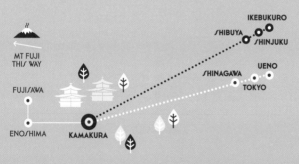

↦ Kamakura Daibutsu at Kotoku-in

TRAIN ACCESS
Catch the JR Shonan Shinjuku line from Ikebukuro, Shibuya or Shinjuku stations, or the JR Sobu Line from Ueno, Tokyo or Shinagawa stations directly to Kamakura. Catch the Eno-den from Fujisawa to Enoshima.

POCKET TIP

Meigetsu-in Temple in Kita Kamakura features a famous view of breathtaking autumn foliage through a circular window.

KAMAKURA SIGHTS

The primary attraction in Kamakura is the spectacular **Kamakura Daibutsu**, a giant brass statue of the Amida Buddha (cast in 1252, it's still the second tallest in Japan) that sits calmly in the grounds of the **Kotokuin Temple** against a backdrop of serene mountains. The streets around Kotokuin are packed with great street food and souvenir buys. Nearby you'll find **Hase-dera**, a temple devoted to the goddess of mercy. Her eleven-headed statue is in the Kannon-do hall. At over nine-metres (and gilded with gold), it's one of Japan's tallest wooden sculptures. Hundreds of tiny Jizo (protective statues) fill the aptly named Jizo-do hall. The grounds are beautiful and from the main buildings there's fabulous views over the town of Kamakura. It's also a favourite photo and picnic spot in sakura (cherry blossom) season with trees strategically planted to frame the main temple. A kilometre away **Koko-kuji** temple has an impressive bamboo grove. Walking in Kamakura's rolling hills or shopping and strolling through the festive streets makes for a perfect day. Kamakura also has several tourist beaches including **Yuigahama** and **Zaimokuza**, where people go to swim, surf and gaze out over the ocean.

KAMAKURA SHOPPING & EATING

The shops and eateries on and around Komachidori (the main street) are enough to keep you busy for a day. Tokyo is known for Hato Sabure, the dove-shaped cookies given as 'omiyage' (holiday gifts) and Kamakura is the birthplace. **Toshimaya Honten**, established in the Meiji era in 1868, has a wide range of beautifully wrapped plump dove merchandise. Fans of Tamagoyaki (Japanese rolled omelette) should head into **Tamagoyaki Gozen**. For vegetarians, a set lunch at **Vegetus** is truly memorable, as is beautiful **Sorafune**, the Kamakura vegetable cafe. **The Bank** is a little bar set up in a 1927 Deco/Nouveau-style (Taisho era) building that once housed the Kamakura Yuigahama bank. Don't miss **Kamakura Beniya**, selling caramel walnut butter cookies and ice-cream emblazoned with their ultra-cute squirrel logo. **Mikawaya Honten** specialises in local sake and craft beers. Sweet lovers head to **Dankazura Kozusu**, where they hand knead warabi mochi in the traditional way. The jelly-like brown sugar and soy flour treat is best enjoyed from the charming upstairs room. Buy Eno-den themed sweets from **Enoden Monaka** or perhaps a model of the train at the station souvenir shop.

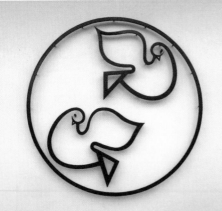

TRAVEL TIPS

GETTING TO TOKYO

Tokyo has two international airports: Narita and Haneda.

NARITA

Narita airport is 71 kilometres from the city. See: narita-airport.jp/en/access

Narita Express Train

Around ¥3000 will get you a one-way ticket to Tokyo station in 53 minutes. Return tickets within a two-week period are discounted. See: jreast.co.jp/e/nex/

Keisei Skyliner Train

For around ¥2500, the Skyliner will take you to Nippori or Ueno stations in around 41 minutes, handy if you are staying near these areas, or near Asakusa. You can transfer to the Yamanote line (*see* p. 185) at Nippori or Ueno; this can get you to Tokyo station in 10 minutes. The Skyliner runs from 8.17am to 10.30pm. See: keisei.co.jp/keisei/tetudou/skyliner/us/ae_outline/index

Keisei Limited Express Train

Around ¥1100 will get you to Ueno, but it will take 71 minutes. If you are on a budget, and patient, this could be a good option. It operates from 5.41am to 10.30pm. See: keisei.co.jp/keisei/tetudou/skyliner/us/nrt_access/tokkyu.php

Tokyo Shuttle

¥1000 with a reservation or ¥1500 without, this bus from Tokyo and Ginza stations is the new bargain way to get to Narita. See: keiseibus.co.jp/inbound/tokyoshuttle/en/

Limousine Bus

Costs ¥3100 and takes around 80 to 100 minutes to get to Tokyo (buses go all over Tokyo). See: limousinebus.co.jp/en/

Taxi

A very expensive option. It will cost you around ¥23,000 and take about 60 to 80 minutes, depending on the traffic, however there are some great shared taxi services for around ¥7,500 per person.

HANEDA

Haneda airport is 22 kilometres from the city. See: haneda-airport.jp/inter/en/access/

Tokyo Monorail

Haneda to Hamamatsucho/Shinagawa station in 13 minutes. See: tokyo-monorail.co.jp/english/

Limousine Bus

It costs ¥1,230 and takes around 35 to 75 minutes to Shinjuku. It costs ¥2,000 at night and runs between midnight and 5am. There can be delays, depending on traffic conditions. See: limousinebus.co.jp/en/

Taxi

Taxis are a very expensive option. It will cost between ¥6,000 and ¥9,000 depending on which part of Tokyo you are staying in.

Limousine and shuttle services

Ask your hotel if they have a specific deal or see: airportlimo-tokyo.com or tokyo-taxi.jp/english/service/index.html

DAYTRIPS

Greater Tokyo Pass

A three-day pass for ¥7200, for details see: greater-tokyo-pass.jp

JR Tokyo Wide Pass

A three-day pass for ¥10,000, for details see: jreast.co.jp/e/tokyowidepass

Japan Rail 7 and 14 day passes

If you are planning on doing quite a few daytrips this may be the pass for you: japanrailpass.net/en

Shinjuku Bus Terminal

Lots of daytrips take off from this terminal. See: highway-buses.jp/terminal/shinjuku.php

GETTING AROUND

Trains

Grab a **Suica** or **Pasmo** card from machines at train stations. For a deposit of around ¥500, these cards are rechargeable and easy to use. Top them up at the machines (they have English instructions) and swipe them at the barrier gates to get into a station. You can also use them on buses, in station lockers, and in an increasing number of vending machines, restaurants and convenience stores.

Train passes

There are also day passes for some of the separate networks: Tokyo Metro and JR are both good options as they have a network of trains in and around all the precincts. Ask at the JR counter at one of the big stations.

Train tips

Know your station exit! It is easy to get lost.

Trains run from around 5am to midnight.

Trains have women-only cars at certain times, and some seats are reserved for the elderly, injured or pregnant. If you are pregnant, you can get a 'maternity badge' at train stations to make other travellers aware and mindful of your condition.

Line up for the trains in designated areas and wait for all other passengers to get off before boarding.

Cram yourself in at peak times; it's one of the few times Tokyoites get up close and very personal.

If you have a train ticket but you're not sure whether it has enough value on it for your journey, you can adjust your fare at a fare-adjustment machine when you get to your destination.

The Yamanote line is a circular line that stops at some of the major stations in Tokyo, and also a few surprising ones (Takadanobaba is the home of Astro Boy, and, as such, plays the Astro Boy theme as its station music). In winter the trains are warm, in summer, cool. Make a day of it! Ride the Yamanote and get off at random stations; you'll find all kinds of cool things.

Trains are great fun, comfortable and often have little TVs playing very cute advertisements to help you pass the time.

Taxis

Taxis cost ¥410 for the first 1.052 kilometres, then ¥200 for every kilometre after that. Late at night, fares can rise by 20%. All tolls will be calculated in the cost of your fare.

Bikes

Riding a bike is a great way to get around a single precinct. You can hire bikes at many places, including **Muji** (*see* p. 73) in Yurakucho, **Tokyo Bike** in Yoyogi Park (*see* p. 18) and **Geographica** (*see* p. 163) in Meguro. You can even hire electric bikes! See: rentabike.jp

Buses

Buses within Tokyo's 23 wards are to be entered from the front. Prices are fixed (usually ¥200), so put your money into the box next to the driver, get a ticket and exit from the rear. If you have a Suica or Pasmo card, it's easiest to swipe it on entry at the front of the bus, then leave at the back.

Walking

You'll do a lot of walking in Tokyo – it's how you'll stumble across some of your best finds – so wear a good pair of shoes! At major crossings, when the pedestrian light turns green, all traffic stops and people go in all directions! It's called 'the scramble' and Shibuya's crossing (*see* p. 2) is the big one. Join in the fun: when the lights change, launch yourself into the chaos. It's estimated that about 1000 people cross at Shibuya at any one time!

A map is your friend in Tokyo. Once you've found the right train station exit, look on your map for identifiable places, like convenience stores, museums or banks, and get your bearings from there. You can also ask at police boxes, or ask a local: they may not speak English but if you have a map or Google Maps, it's likely they'll walk you to your destination no matter how far out of their way they have to go.

ELECTRONICS

Tokyo has great electronic gadgets and devices, but remember that they are a different wattage and the power plugs use different outlets. If you really have to buy something, you'll need to get it converted or buy a transformer device. Some stores will sell Western versions, which have already been changed over. Duty-free places at the airport will have Western-style wattage.

PHONES & WI-FI

To access wi-fi in Tokyo, you have a few options. Many travellers rent pocket wi-fi at Narita airport to use with their smart phone. You can also hire a mobile phone at the airport, or buy a SIM card for your phone; at outlets around the city such as SoftBank or Docomo, Tokyo's major mobile phone providers.

7-Eleven stores have free wi-fi, as do Loft stores, the Yamanote train line and Tokyo Metro. Check online for some great new apps to download before you leave that find hotspots for you. Information at Hikarie Shibuya (*see* p. 10) will set you up with 'Visit Shibuya', a week of free wi-fi for Shibuya hotspots (you'll need your passport).

Grab a pocket wi-fi at one of the many counters at the airport or at a Bic Camera in the city, or hook up an inexpensive plan from home. If you search for pocket wi-fi online you'll see the myriad of choices, many have cheaper deals if you book online. Some hotels now provide pocket wi-fi or a smart phone in the room so remember to ask before you book, it may make a difference to your choice.

To call somewhere outside of Tokyo, dial 010, then the country code of where you're calling, and then the area code, dropping the initial '0'.

Tokyo's area code is 03, but you don't need to dial it if you're calling within Tokyo.

It's considered rude to talk on your mobile phone on trains.

SHOPPING

When you enter a shop (or restaurant), staff will say 'irrashaimase', which means, you are welcome. There's not really an answer to this, but sometimes it's so emphatic you'll feel like saying something in return! Just say 'konnichiwa' (hello).

SHOPPING TIPS

Carry your passport with you so that if you purchase something worth over ¥10,000 in major department stores or stores that have a tax-free sign, it can be bought duty free.

Do not haggle in Tokyo, unless you are at an open-air market.

MONEY

Japan's currency is the yen, denoted by ¥.

It comes in denominations of ¥1000, ¥2000, ¥5000 and ¥10,000 in notes, and ¥1, ¥5, ¥10, ¥50, ¥100 and ¥500 in coins. The ¥5 and ¥50 coins have holes in the middle of them.

There is an 8 per cent consumption tax in Japan. It is sometimes included in the price of things, but often isn't, so check first. Sometimes a 'service charge' is also added, so for hotels and restaurants this can really stack up. Make sure you're aware of any additional costs like this before purchasing something.

Not all ATMs take international cards, so if you need to get extra cash, look for a **Seven Bank**, which will always accept them. You'll find Seven Banks in **7-Elevens** and in separate outlets.

Some large stores and department stores have international ATMs. Main post offices also have international ATMs.

USEFUL WORDS & PHRASES

Pronunciation is simply this: vowels are 'a' (pronounced like the 'u' in up), 'i' (pronounced like the 'i' in imp), 'u' (pronounced as the 'oo' in book), 'e' (pronounced as the 'e' in egg) and 'o' (pronounced as the 'o' in lock). This doesn't change for any word, and if two vowels are placed together, you say them as if they were separate vowel sounds in a row. Simple! The letter 'r' is pronounced as a cross between an 'r' and an 'l'; the easiest way to make this sound is to touch the roof of your mouth with the tip of your tongue.

Useful Kanji

Tokyo: 東京
Japan: 日本
Yen: 円
Male: 男
Female: 女
Enter: 入口
Exit: 出口
North: 北
South: 南
East: 東
West: 西

Try and memorise the kanji for Tokyo; it's especially useful for reading the weather on television. Male and female kanji is also useful for toilet signage in some restaurants and cafes.

Do you speak English?: anata wa eigo o hanashimasu ka?
I don't understand: wakarimasen
I don't understand Japanese: Nihongo ga wakarimasen
Hello: konnichiwa
Good morning: ohayou gozaimasu
Goodnight: oyasuminasai
Goodbye: sayonara
See you later: mata ne
Nice to meet you: hajimemashite
Please: kudasai/onegaishimasu
Thank you: arigato, arigato gozaimasu
Thank you very much: domo arigato
Excuse me: sumimasen
How are you?: genki desu ka?
I'm well: genki desu or genki
How much is this?: ikura desu ka?
I'll take this: kore kudasai
Cheers!: kanpai!
I would like a beer please: biru wo kudasai (or add nama before biru for a draught beer)
Delicious: oishii
Can I have the bill please?: okanjo onegaishimasu?
After eating a delicious meal say: gochisousama deshita
Train station: eki
Airport: kuukou
Taxi: takushi
I love Japan!: Watashi wa Nihon ga daisuki!

HOTEL RECOMMENDATIONS

Capsules
Shibuya (Female Only), President Spa Resort (Male Only), 9 hours, Hotel Siesta, Nadeshiko Hotel

Hostels
Nui Hostel and Bar Lounge, GRIDS Akihabara Hotel & Hostel

Well priced
Omo Hotel, Book and Bed

Approved chains
Dormy Inn, Remm, Mitsui Garden

Boutique
The Gate, Granbell, Claska, Trunk Hotel, Park Hotel

Beautiful
Hotel Okura, Tokyo Station Hotel, Aman

Out of this world Ryokan experiences
Hoshinoya Tokyo

Ryokan
Homeikan Ryokan, Asakusa Shigetsu, Kimi Ryokan, Takemine, Andon Ryokan

EATING OUT

Make sure you check the opening hours of your desired cafe or restaurant. Most cafes and bars shut for one day during the week, and many cafes open around 11am or 12pm.

It's good fun to try the omakase (chef's choice) at restaurants. The chefs decide what they think is the best choice for you.

If you don't speak Japanese, ask your hotel to make restaurant reservations on your behalf. Most places are licensed.

Lunch starts at 11.30am and finishes between 2 and 3pm.

Set lunches are great value, especially at places that do an expensive dinner.

When using chopsticks, don't stick them upright in a bowl of rice – this is a funeral custom. Also, don't pass food to, or take food from, other people using chopsticks, and don't spear food with them (okay, we may have done this a few times …). Lastly, don't use chopsticks to move a bowl towards you.

It is customary to pour other people's drinks.

Many small eateries have plastic food models out the front of their establishment, and many cafes have pictorial menus, which is very handy if you don't speak Japanese. You can show a staff member the menu, point to your preferred dish and say either 'onegaishimasu' (polite) or 'okudasai' – two Japanese words for 'please'.

Tipping is not a thing in Tokyo. In fact, it will cause confusion.

CONVENIENCE STORES

Tokyo's convenience stores, or konbinis, are awesome. You might be used to convenience stores having higher prices for junky products, but in Tokyo they are fast, cheap, convenient and sell great stuff, including cheap beer, fresh fruit and vegetables, sweets, magazines and delicious take-away food. Sometimes they have their own select ranges, and FamilyMarts stock Muji products. You can even buy concert and museum tickets. We could happily do a convenience-store tour of Tokyo. Sunkus, FamilyMart, Lawson, AM/PM and 7-Eleven are the main stores, but look out for cute neighbourhood versions too.

VENDING MACHINES

Vending machines are everywhere. The variety of drinks they have is staggering – convenient if you want a hot green tea or coffee in winter or cold drink at any time of the year. They can also sell anything from hamburgers to toilet paper, stationery, shirts, alcohol and cup noodles.

MANNERS

Manners are very important in Japan, so always be as polite as possible. Invoke your inner sense of calm and treat everyone with respect, and respect will be returned to you. The deeper someone bows, the more respect they are showing you. Most younger people don't bow as much now, but a slight bow of the head is always a good thing.

Take off your shoes before getting onto a tatami mat or entering a house. A lot of restaurants will also require you to remove your shoes, but the staff will let you know. There are usually slippers provided, but these are for going to the bathroom (you don't have to worry about this in more contemporary restaurants). You should even take your shoes off when entering a clothing-store changing room.

If you're sick with a cold, buy a face mask. Also, don't take a wet umbrella into a shop; use the bags or holders provided. (Note: grab a clear plastic umbrella from konbinis or stands at the train stations if it's raining; they are cheap and well made.)

Crime is low in Tokyo. There are very few dangerous areas. Honestly, you could drop your wallet and someone will pick it up and give it back to you, or if you left it somewhere, it will likely be mailed to you.

TOILETS

Public toilets are easy to find and range from the basic to the so-intricate that you'll never have time to work out all of the functions. Some toilets play music, so pick a tune! The nicest toilets are located in department stores. Some public toilets are non-Western (squat) ones, so beware, or dare!

ADDRE//E/

Even Tokyoites have trouble with the city's address system – they use maps as well! Always consult a map, and navigate using nearby landmarks, shrines or convenience stores.

A typical Tokyo addresss will read like this: 5-35-1 Daita Setagaya. In order, the numbers stand for subsection (ward), block number and then building number. In Tokyo, the ground floor is referred to as the first floor (1F; the next floor up is 2F), and the floor beneath that is the basement. There's no point looking for street names as most streets don't have names! The ones that do were mostly named by the Americans after World War Two to help them get around.

PUBLIC HOLIDAY/ & FE/TIVAL/

Christmas Day is a normal working day in Tokyo. Christmas night is considered 'date night' in Japan, especially for the young.

New Year is the big holiday in Japan. Celebrations involve visits to shrines to pray for good fortune and health in the coming year. Businesses can close the week before New Year, and stay shut for the first few weeks of January. Check attractions before you visit.

Golden Week starts on 29 April and extends into the first week of May. Book your accommodation well in advance at this time.

NERIMA-KU

NAKANO-KU

MUSASHINO-SHI

209 —

⊕ 20,000
DEN
ATSU

— 208

SUGINAMI-KU

SUNDAY
BAKE SHOP

MITAKA-SHI

東京
TOKYO

199 —

198 —

192-3

CHOFU-SHI

SETAGAYA-KU

BC
AND SC

KOMAE-SHI

KAWASAKI-SHI

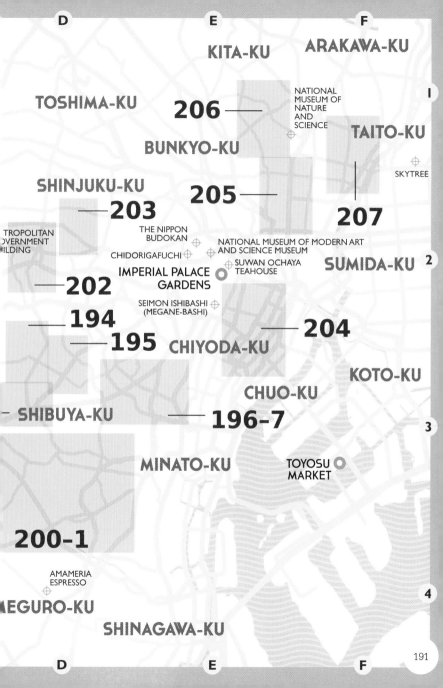

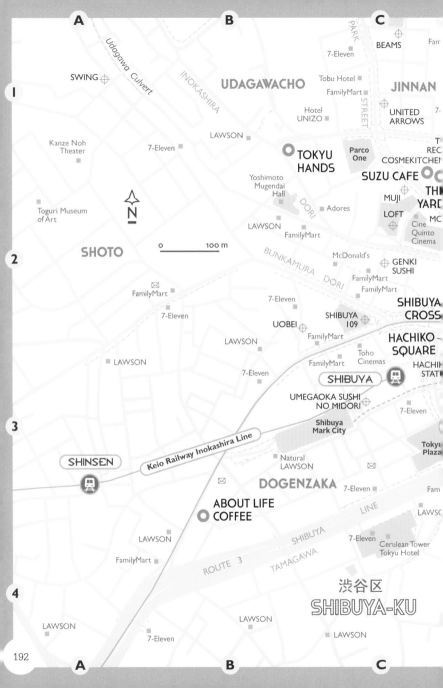

A   B   C

I

Udagawa Culvert

SWING ⊕

INOKASHIRA

UDAGAWACHO

7-Eleven

BEAMS

Fam

Tobu Hotel ■

FamilyMart ■

JINNAN

PARK

STREET

Kanze Noh
Theater
■

7-Eleven ■

LAWSON ■

Hotel
UNIZO ■

⊕ **UNITED
ARROWS**

7-

TOKYU
HANDS ○

Parco
One

T
REC
COSMEKITCHEN

Toguri Museum
of Art
■

N

Yoshimoto
Mugendai
Hall
■

SUZU CAFE ○ C

MUJI ■

⊕ **THE
YARD**

SHOTO

0   100 m

DORI

■ Adores

LOFT ■

Cine
Quinto
Cinema

MC

LAWSON ■

FamilyMart ■

2

BUNKAMURA DORI

McDonald's ■

⊕ **GENKI
SUSHI**

FamilyMart ■

FamilyMart ■

☒
FamilyMart ■

7-Eleven ■

7-Eleven ■

UOBEI ⊕

SHIBUYA
109 ⊕

**SHIBUYA
CROSS**

FamilyMart ■

**HACHIKO ~
SQUARE**

LAWSON ■

Toho
Cinemas ■

**HACHII
STATI**

FamilyMart ■

SHIBUYA 🚇

7-Eleven ■

7-Eleven ■

UMEGAOKA SUSHI
NO MIDORI ⊕

3

SHINSEN 🚇

Keio Railway Inokashira Line

Shibuya
Mark City ■

7-Eleven ■

Natural
LAWSON ■

☒

Toku
Plaza

■ LAWSON

☒

DOGENZAKA 7-Eleven ■

Fam

LAWSON ■

**ABOUT LIFE
COFFEE** ○

LINE

LAWSC

LAWSON ■

SHIBUYA

7-Eleven ■

Cerulean Tower
Tokyu Hotel ■

FamilyMart ■

ROUTE 3

TAMAGAWA

4

渋谷区
SHIBUYA-KU

LAWSON
■

LAWSON
■

LAWSON
■

7-Eleven ■

A   B   C

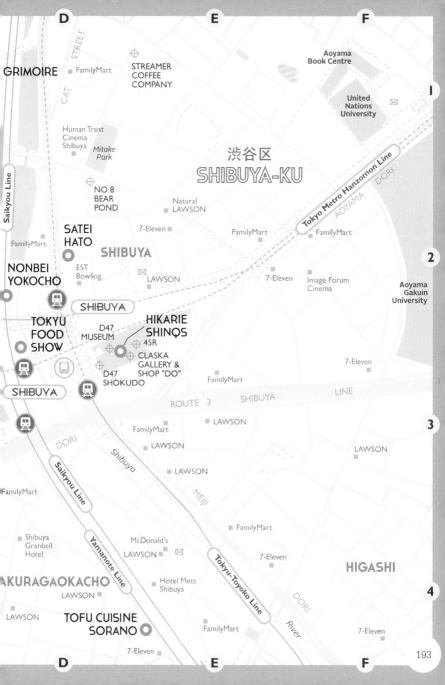

A
B
C

1

MEIJI
JINGŪ

Meiji Shrine
Kaguraden

Meiji
Jingū
Hall

JINGUMAE

7-Eleven

PLAYMOUNTAIN

MEIJI DORI

DORI

Meiji Shrine
Sanshuden

Forest
Terrace
Meiji
Shrine

N

0   100 m

2

YOYOGI
PARK

South
Pond

Saikyou Line

FamilyMart

McDonald's

Takeshita
Dori

7-Eleven

Togo
Shrine

Kamiike
Pond

LAWSON

FamilyMart

渋谷区
SHIBUYA-KU

DORI

Tokyo Metro Chiyoda Line

Jingu Bashi
(Shrine Bridge)

HARAJUKU

OMOTESANDO

Ota Memorial
Museum of Art

McDonald's

MEIJI-JINGUMAE

3

DORI

Yamanote Line

INOKASHIRA

LAWSON

THE
GYRE
BUILDING

KIDDY LAND

YOYOGI
NATIONAL
GYMNASIUM

HARAJUKU GYOZA-RO

Alice on
Wednesday

LUKE'S LOBSTER

CAT STREET

FRED
PERRY

AVENUE OF
ZELKOVA
TREES

STREET

WARA
TAKO

ART STYLE
MARKET

RAGTAG

STREET

NHK
Theatre

AiiA 2.5
Theater
Tokyo

JOURNAL
STANDARD

FIRE

Premium
Dormy Inn
Hotel

MEIJI

CAT

THE ROASTERY
BY NOZY COFFEE

BULLE DE SAVON

4

G.B
GAFAS

SOT

194

A

JINNAN

B

FamilyMart

C

D **E** **F** **I**

Okura Museum of Art
(Okura Shukokan)

Suntory
Hall

Hotel
Okura
Tokyo   7-Eleven   ■ Musée
Tomo

7-Eleven

ROPPONGI-ITCHOME

LAWSON

Hotel Villa
Fontaine
Roppongi

Natural
LAWSON

7-Eleven

McDonald's

7-Eleven

ROPPONGI

TORANOMON

KAMIYACHO

FamilyMart

FamilyMart

2

7-Eleven

Yoshida Hochiku ■
Memorial Hall

7-Eleven

ilyMart

LAWSON

GAIEN   HIGASHI

Diplomatic Archives
(Ministry of Foreign Affairs)

7-Eleven

3

UGUISU
THE LITTLE
SHOPPE

TOKYO ⊕ ■ One
TOWER   Piece
Tower

LAWSON ■

**TOFU
UKAI**

HIGASHIAZBU

AZABU-JUBAN

FamilyMart   Natural
LAWSON

NANIWAYA
SOHONTEN

LAWSON

4

eleven

McDonald's

DORI   Toei Oedo Line

AZABU-JUBAN

AKABANEBASHI

ichan
ue

D   7-Eleven   **E**   **F**

Tokyo Metro Nanboku Line

INNER CIRCLE ROUTE

IZUMI

SAKURADA   DORI

Tokyo Metro Hibiya Line

DORI

INNER CIRCLE

SAKURADA

IYAIDA
DORI

DORI

A
B
C

LAWSON ✉

LAWSON

■ FamilyMart

KITAZAWA

HAIGHT &
ASHBURY ○

DORI

I

NOUMIN
ORGANIC
CAFE ○

JET SET
RECORDS ○

LAWSON ■

Kitazawa
Town Hall
■

7-Eleven ■

CHAZAWA

Keio Railway Inokashira Line

SHIMO-KITAZAWA

LAWSON

🚉

Hondagekijiyo ■

McDonald's
■

2

BIO
OJIYAN
CAFE ○

○ CITY
COUNTRY
CITY

7-Eleven ■

FOG
LINEN
WORK ○

Odakyu Odawara Line

世田谷区
SETAGAYA-KU

DORI

DARWIN
ROOM ○

DAIZAWA

3

⌂
N

FamilyMart
■

✉

7-Eleven ■

CHAZAWA

0   100 m

DAITA

Shinganji
Temple

Kitazawa
Hachiman
Shrine

4

DASHIN
SOAN
SOBA ○

198

A
B
C

A

SHOKUAN DORI

B

DORI

LAWSON

C

Okubo Park
Premier Hotel Cabin Shinjuku
7-Eleven

HIGASHI-SHINJUKU

FamilyMart

Shinjuku Eastside Business Park

FamilyMart

Shinjuku Granbell Hotel

SEIBU-SHINJUKU

1

KABUKICHO

KUYAKUSHO DORI

Shinjuku Bunka Center

TATSUNOYA

RAMEN JIRO

MENYA MUSASHI

7-Eleven

7-Eleven

LAWSON

7-Eleven

Kabukicho

FamilyMart

7-Eleven

Godzilla Head

7-Eleven

FamilyMart

LAWSON

GOLDEN GAI

FamilyMart

McDonald's

CALICO CAT

ALBATROSS G

Shinjuku Sunlite Hotel

7-Eleven

SUGOI NIBOSHI RAMEN NAGI & BAR PLASTIC MODEL

7-Eleven

7-Eleven

Yunika Vision

TOKYO IDAI DOR

2

Chuo Line

LAWSON

LAWSON

FamilyMart

DUG

YASUKUNI

FamilyMart

Shinjuku Piccadilly (cinema)

NAKAMURAYA CAFE

SHINJUKU

MEIJI

7-Eleven

FamilyMart

SHINJUKU

ISETAN

LAWSON

TEMPURA TSUNAHACHI

SHINJUKU

LAWSON

SHINJUKU-SANCHOME

LAWSON

DISC UNION

DORI FamilyMart

Shinjuku Information Center

SAMURAI

7-Eleven

FamilyMart

SHINJUKU

3

NEWOMAN

BLUE BOTTLE COFFEE

KOSHU

McDonald's

7-Eleven

新宿区

SHINJUKU-KU

TORAYA CAFE

Times Square Shopping Plaza

MEIJI

KAIDO

FamilyMart

Sunroute Plaza Shinjuku Hotel

TSUKEMEN GONOKAMI SEISAKUSHO

N

7-Eleven

Upper Pond

RAKUUTEI

SHINJUKU GYOEN

4

SHOUTENTEI

DORI

0   200 m

7-Eleven

YOYOGI

A

B

C

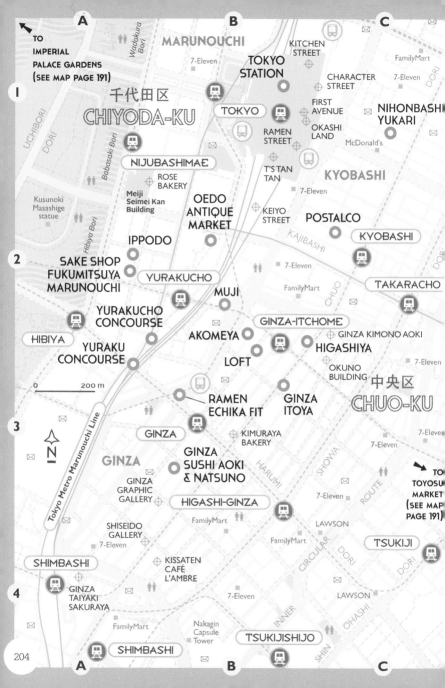

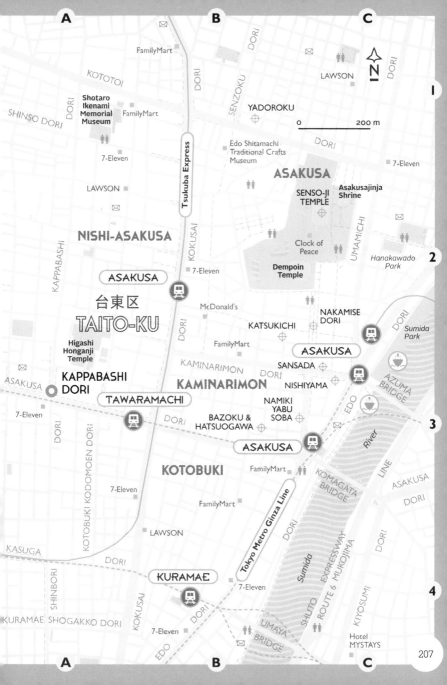

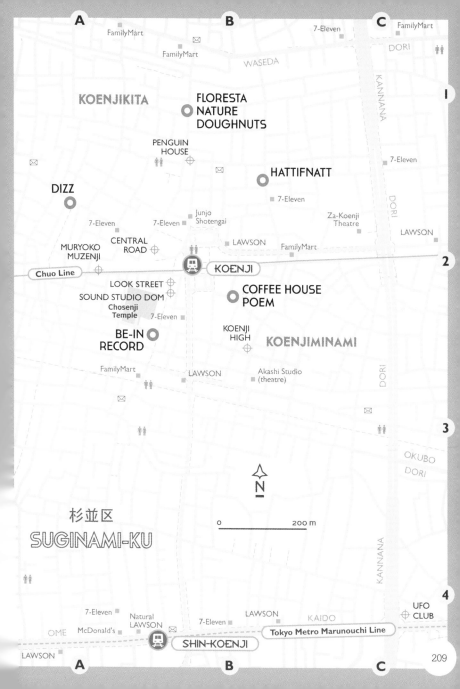

A
B
C

FamilyMart

7-Eleven

FamilyMart

DORI

FamilyMart

FamilyMart

WASEDA

KANNANA

I

KOENJIKITA

FLORESTA
NATURE
DOUGHNUTS

PENGUIN
HOUSE

7-Eleven

HATTIFNATT

DORI

DIZZ

7-Eleven

Junjo
Shotengai

Za-Koenji
Theatre

7-Eleven

LAWSON

7-Eleven

7-Eleven

LAWSON

CENTRAL
ROAD

LAWSON

FamilyMart

MURYOKO
MUZENJI

Chuo Line

KOENJI

2

LOOK STREET

COFFEE HOUSE
POEM

SOUND STUDIO DOM

Chosenji
Temple

7-Eleven

KOENJI
HIGH

KOENJIMINAMI

BE-IN
RECORD

DORI

FamilyMart

LAWSON

Akashi Studio
(theatre)

3

OKUBO
DORI

N

杉並区
SUGINAMI-KU

0   200 m

KANNANA

4

UFO
CLUB

7-Eleven

Natural
LAWSON

LAWSON

KAIDO

OME

McDonald's

7-Eleven

Tokyo Metro Marunouchi Line

LAWSON

SHIN-KOENJI

A
B
C

INDEX

INDEX